The Great Silencing of British Working Class Culture

SILENCE!

A ranting, singing, picture book by

Stefan Szczelkun

Short title Silence!

Book data: 165 x 165mm 105 gsm paper standard colour by Ingramspark.com

ISBN 978-1-870736-22-0

Distributor - **Central Books,** London

Published by

Routine Art Co

London 2020

Cover design by Chris Saunders

Foreword

At a moment when working class culture seems to have been overtaken by issues of national identity, this book comes as a timely reminder of where the roots of most of the UK's population lie. It is brought to life by Stefan Szczelkun's own recollections of his post-war upbringing and insightful observations on the significance of music, singing, amateur film and other popular forms as cultural expression of this much vilified though predominant social class. Creatively presented as a collage of ideas, references and images, this book is as much visual artefact as rigorous research, and makes for an intriguing and engaging reading experience.

Lorraine Leeson

- My hypothesis is repression of working class culture must happen whenever urbanisation reaches a certain intensity.

- When enough working-class people are close together in great numbers they have potential for solidarity and a power as yet unrealised. That power flowers through cultural play - yes, at the core of this idea is mucking about and having a laugh. Or to use another word, 'improvisation'.

- Class oppression is imposed from 'above' through the media, education and through other cultural institutions. We kick back against it intuitively but not in an organised way. Not 'as a class'!

- Becoming aware of how cultural oppression is imposed is half way to throwing off its mental shackles. I will continue by talking about the situation I have lived with in the UK.

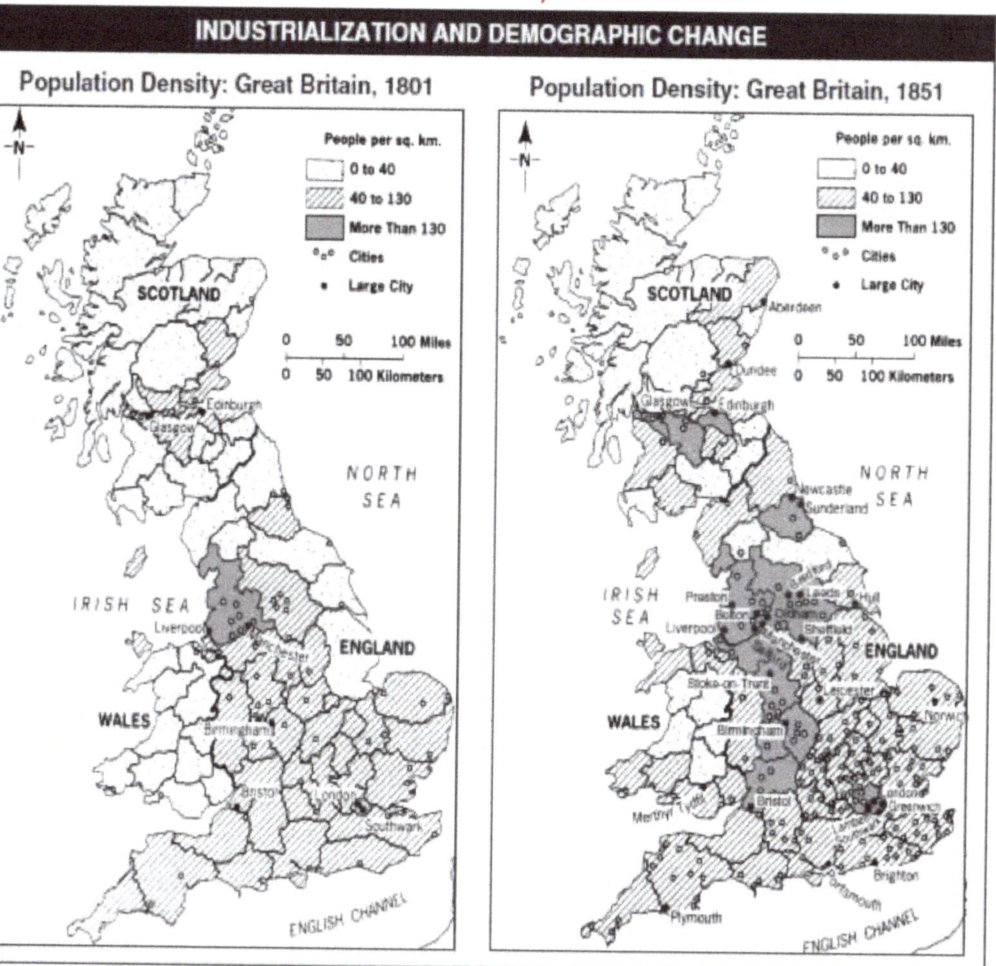

Source: *World Civilizations: Sources, Images, and Interpretations,* McGraw-Hill (adapted)

Moving into towns.

How did people's lives change?

- It is perhaps hard for us urbanites to imagine the radical change of lifestyle, that moving to a town for the first time, required. The yearly cycles are all but gone, the mythical richness of nature becomes a fading memory.

- The exciting new thing about cities was living so closely together. It was so much more *intense!* More talking, more social action to excite all the senses - 'havin' a laff' with intent.

- The upper classes couldn't keep an eye on what was going on as easily as they used to in the country. This caused the establishment to fear the ebullience of the new urban 'masses'.

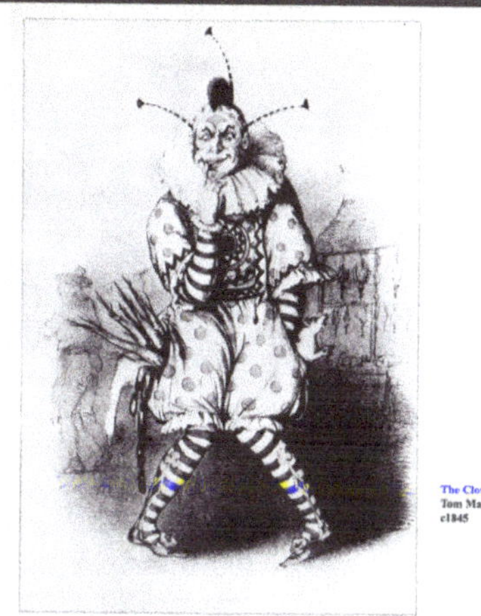

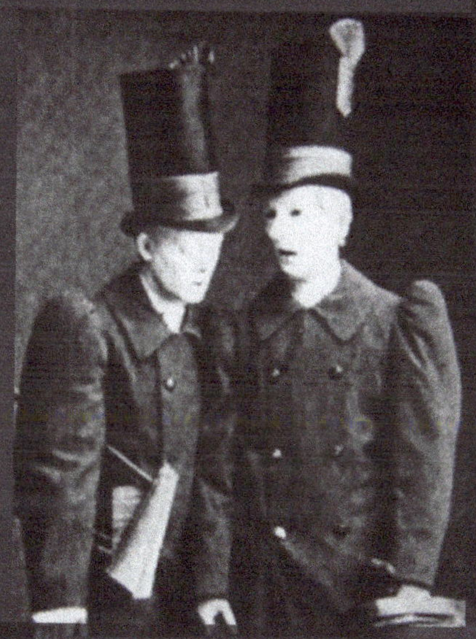

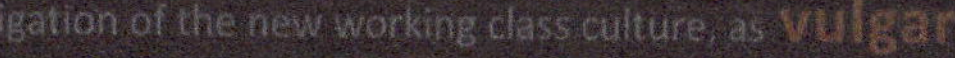
igation of the new working class culture, as **vulgar**

lgarity!

In chapter 5 of his 2013 book '**Aesthesis,**' Jacques Rancière discusses the English physical comedians of the C19th music-hall. They have no relation to literary narrative. They were breaking the bounds of normal theatrical representation with illusions of 'impossible action'. This lack of representation of status or moral purpose suggests that this form was a precursor of a democratic modernity in which culture does not have a didactic purpose, it is not there to raise one up. Life has a 'lack of reason' in our daily experience of it. The English comic mimes follow the 'twists and turns' of this lack of logical progression. In their hands it is an essential knot of poetic dream and gymnastic performance. Rancière uses Theodore de Banville's description of a highly-rated English 'pantomime' group, the Hanlon-Lees Brothers:

"The absurdity of situations lacking any motivation; the instant passage from the most absolute immobility to the violent exuberance of gestures that multiply blows in every direction and make bodies fly across space; finally, the use of the tricks that allow bodies to appear and disappear at any moment, pass through walls, windows, or mirrors, run beheaded after their heads, and make the missing heads appear in the most unlikely places" p.77.

"Poetry itself is the ideal artifice that negates the social education in gravity." p.79
"Pantomime is an anti-theatre, or a theatre cleansed of all the academicism of tragedy as it is of the bourgeois vulgarity of melodrama or comedy of manners, reduced to its ideal essence, in which the exact materiality of the performance is conflated with spectacular ideality accepted as such" p.80.
Of course there were moves to 'modernise' or rationalise the pantomime. To give it characters and conventional order, but this finds "a counter-model in the extravagant cruelty of English mimes … Tom Matthews and his English colleagues" create a violent and "disturbing intrusion onto the bourgeois stage of Varieties" p.86. The effect was macabre as much as it was comic, at a time when Jean-Martin Charcot was investigating deranged 'hysterics' in France and laying the foundations of modern psychology.

Rancière refers to the 'epileptic' pantomime seen and described by Charles Baudelaire in his 1855 essay 'On the Essence of Laughter':

"I shall long remember the first English pantomime that I saw . . . It seemed to me that the distinguishing characteristic of this genre of comedy was violence . . . The English Pierrot was by no means this character pale as the moon, mysterious as silence, supple and mute as the serpent, lean and long as a pole, to which we were accustomed by Deburau. The English Pierrot comes in like a whirlwind, falls like a bale and, when he laughs, he makes the room shake; his laughter sounds like joyful thunder. He is a short, thick fellow, who has increased his bulk by a costume filled with ribbons. On his whitened face he has crudely plastered - without gradation or transition - two enormous slabs of pure red. His mouth is made longer by a simulated prolongation of the lips in the form of two carmine strokes, so that when he laughs, his mouth seems to open from ear to ear . . . His moral nature is basically the same as that of the Pierrot we know: insouciance and neutrality, leading to the realisation of all the rapacious and gluttonous desires, to the detriment sometimes of Harlequin, and sometimes of Cassandre or Léandre. But where Deburau thrust in the point of his finger so that he might afterwards lick it, the clown thrusts in both hands and both feet, and this may express all that he does: his is the vertigo of hyperbole. This English Pierrot passes by a woman who is washing her doorstep: after emptying her pockets, he seeks to cram into his own the sponge, the broom, the soap, and even the water ... Because of the peculiar talent of the English actors for hyperbole, all these monstrous farces take on a strangely gripping reality." translation by John Towsen

In theatre, this leads to Meyerhold's bio-mechanical gymnastic exercises. And in the new film medium, Charles Chaplin, Buster Keaton and Harold Lloyd all refine and add to these techniques with the technical possibilities of film.
"The children of the music-hall who went into the cinema guaranteed it a better-defined and more lasting lineage" p.91.

A do-it-Yourself culture

- The middle class swiftly moved from fear of the masses to exerting control. The established literary middle class saw their culture as superior to oral cultures.

- They began by castigating the new urban musical efflorescence as vulgar and offensive at every opportunity. And by getting control of the newspapers.

- By commercialising the venues of working class culture and using municipal regulations, they could gradually exert control of what went on.

- There was a gradual ordering of the audience as seated, passive and paying, as the commercialisation of popular entertainment spread.

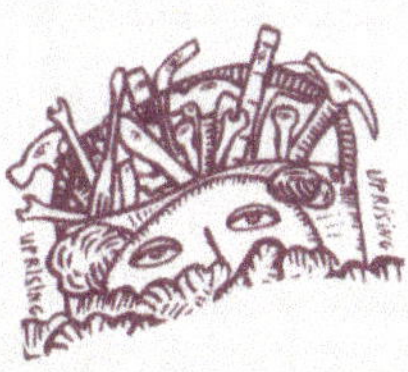

See my pamphlet: 'Kennington Park - the birthplace of British democracy' Present Tense, 2015

1851 - 1901

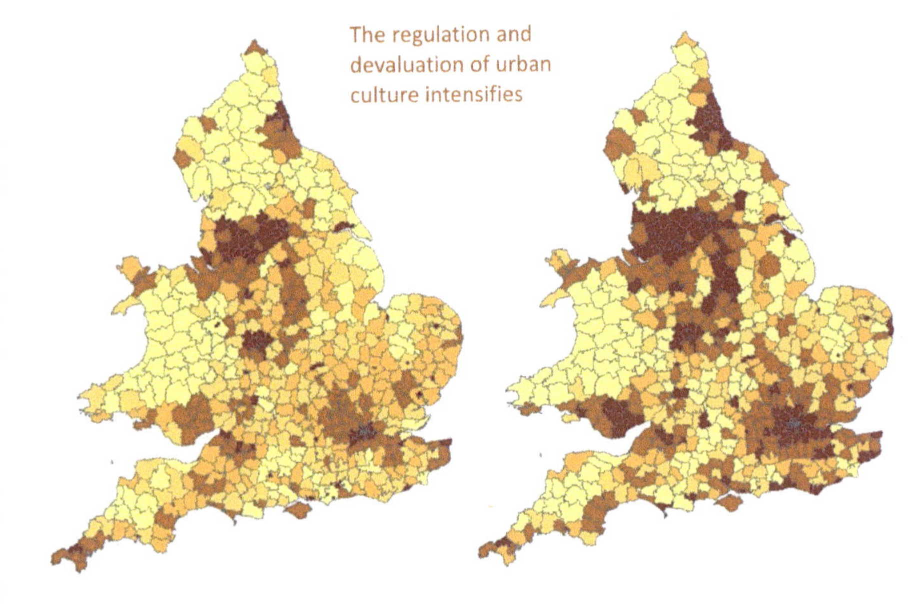

The regulation and
devaluation of urban
culture intensifies

1850

- By 1850 more people were living in towns than countryside in Britain (c2005 that shift occurred globally).

- The radical displacement this entailed from being embedded in nature to urban conditions of living. +

- The represention of the new urban culture that was emerging in free'n'easies, then in purpose made music-halls, as **vulgar and worthless.**

- My hypothesis is that this is an ongoing global phenomenon in urbanising populations. **What is commonly depicted is poverty but the cultural innovations go unseen.**

- 10th April 1848. The Chartist Monster Rally on Kennington Common demanded the vote. It was punished by the enclosure of the common. The new Unions seem not to have recognised cultural oppression or to have defended the culture of their members. (Altho' the Chartists did...)

- The established literary middle class saw themselves and their culture as superior and it was they who owned and controlled the media which promoted *their* values and demeaned other cultures as inferior and existing beneath them.

"**If** one thinks of the outer circumference of our terribly overgrown towns where the jerry-builder holds sway; where one sees all around the tawdriness of sham jewellery and shoddy clothes, pawnshops and flaming gin-palaces; where stale fish and the Covent Garden refuse which pass for vegetables are offered for food - all such things suggest to one's mind the boundless regions of sham.

It is for the people who live in these unhealthy regions - people who, for the most part have the most false ideals, or none at all ... It is for them that the modern popular music is made, and it is made with a commercial intention out of snippets of musical slang!"

Sir Hubert Parry (27 February 1848 – 7 October 1918)

Meanwhile back in the London suburbs in the Fifties.... My family
had this picture up on the wall of the outside toilet. Which gave ample
opportunity for contemplation of where we had come from.

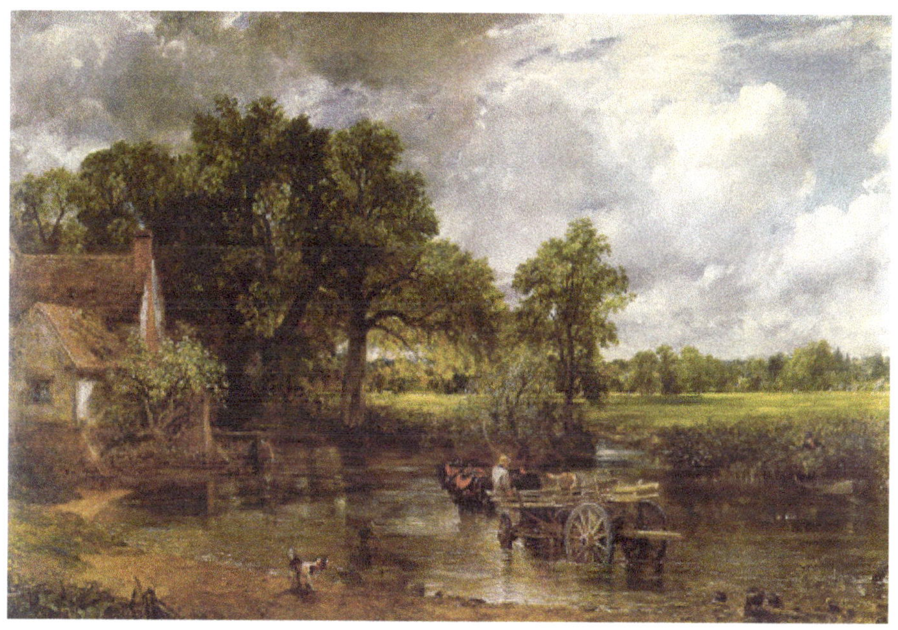

The Haywain by John Constable   1821

- As people left the countryside, gentlemen had collected up their 'discarded' songs, like dried flowers, and preserved them in printed books. Their music was transcribed for the piano 'sol-fa' scales and the lyrics were 'cleaned up' before being fixed in print. One collector in particular had seen the potential of this material in forming a deferential national identity for the masses.

- His name was **Cecil Sharp**.

With the guidance of Sharp and others, bowdlerised versions of rural songs were to be fed back to urban working-class people. Presented to them as their own **'national' culture.**

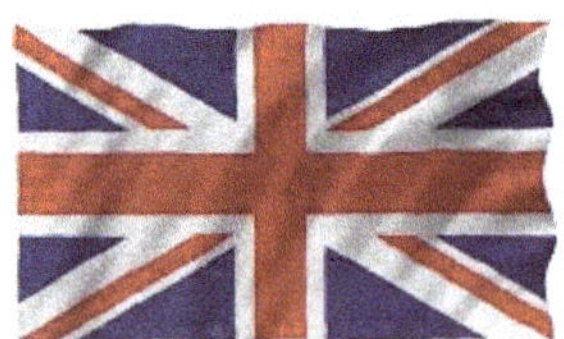

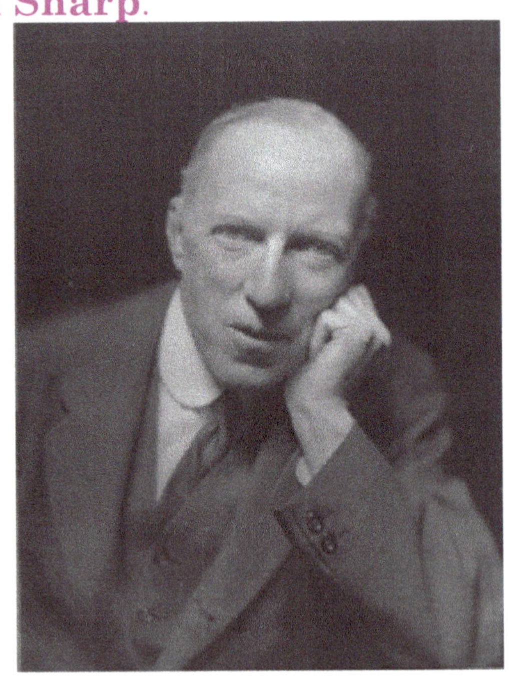

The National Songbook that came out in 1905 and was a selection of songs by The Board of Education, the President of which was the old Etonian Charles Vane Tempest Stewart, the Marquess of Londonderry. His family home was in Machynlleth in mid-Wales although later in life, as a mine owner, he had a seat in County Durham called 'Wynyard Park'. I have not been able to find the names of other members of the Board of Education, who contributed their suggestions for a national(ist) repertoire.

The selection was then edited and arranged for the use of state schools by the eminent **Charles Villiers Standford** who was a professor of music at Cambridge and a successful composer who was only later eclipsed by his students such as Gustav Holst and Vaughn Williams. Williams himself collected folk songs in the period 1903 - 1904 and knew Cecil Sharp.

These 'national' songs were promoted through the new state education system and the book was in use for many years. Local friend Nigel's auntie was using it at the end of the thirties and forties and George Redgrave, known to me through a photosharing website, had the book in the early fifties and still enjoys singing from it. After WW2 and the ubiquity of BBC radio, the promotion of this repertoire was taken over by **BBC for Schools** programmes and publications, which gradually evolved into the seventies. Many of the songs used are embedded in the heads of those of us who grew up in this period.

The idea was to create a national identity by a process of selecting popular patriotic British songs. There are selections of Welsh, Irish and Scottish as well as English songs. So they would have been compelled to include Burns in some form, and there are in fact several Burns songs: *Ca the Ewes to the Knowes, Afton Water, Here Awa' There Awa', Scots Wha Hae Wi' Wallace Bled, Robin Adair, Ye Banks and Braes O' Bonnie Doon,* (as well as a few songs by Burns' contemporary, the amazing Lady Carolina Nairne and *Bonnie Dundee* by Sir Walter Scott.) Burns would have had a name as a song collector and been known, and respected, by composers such as Stanford.

Charles Villiers Stanford believed in two distinct cultural roots, namely the Saxon and Celtic, and four distinct styles:

- English - strong, solid and straightforward

- Welsh - full of dash and 'go'

- Scots - a mixture of humour and poetry

- Irish - with the most remarkable literature of folk music in the world. (Stanford had researched Irish music in some detail)

- He recommended that schools should use national songs as the basis of their teaching, starting with music indigenous to each ethnic group - "the English should only learn English folk songs, the Scots Scottish songs, and so on. Only later should they explore traditions of neighbouring groups."

The Construction of Nationalism

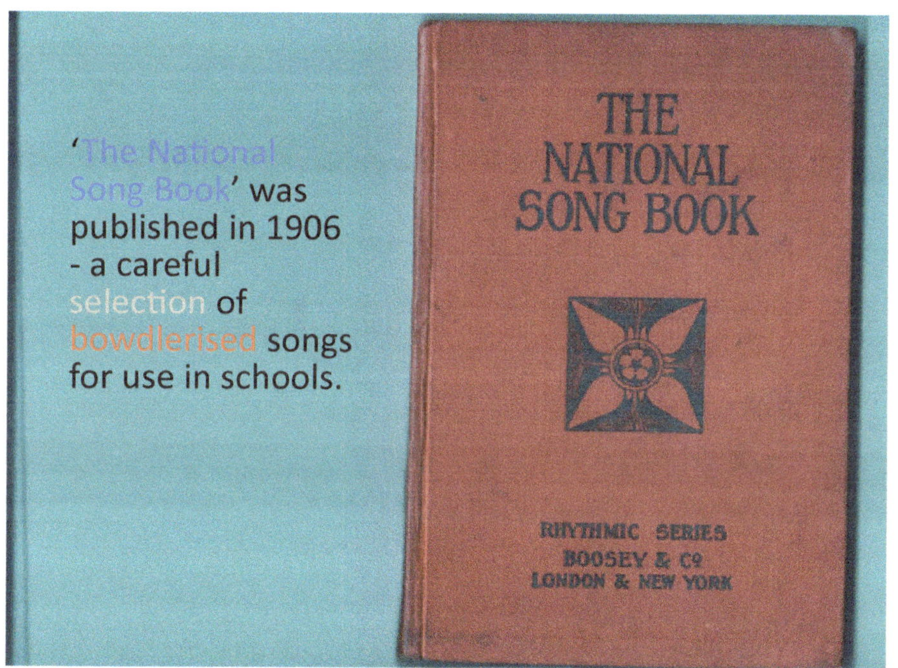

By the start of the First World War there was hardly a school in the country which did not possess a copy.

THE

NATIONAL SONG BOOK

A COMPLETE COLLECTION

OF THE

FOLK-SONGS, CAROLS, AND ROUNDS,

SUGGESTED BY

THE BOARD OF EDUCATION

(1905).

EDITED AND ARRANGED

FOR THE USE OF SCHOOLS

BY

CHARLES VILLIERS STANFORD.

WORDS AND VOICE PARTS ONLY.
(*In Old Notation and Tonic Sol-fa.*)
Ninepence Net.
In Cloth, One Shilling Net.

ENGLISH SONGS *only*, 3d. NET.   IRISH SONGS *only*, 3d. NET.
SCOTCH SONGS ,, 3d. NET.   WELSH SONGS ,, 3d. NET.
CAROLS, ROUNDS, AND CATCHES, TWOPENCE NET.

COMPLETE, FOR VOICE AND PIANOFORTE, 3/- NET.
IN LIMP COVER, GILT, 4/6 NET.

WORDS ONLY, SIXPENCE NET.

BOOSEY & CO.,

295, REGENT STREET, LONDON, W.,

And 9, EAST 17th STREET, NEW YORK.

Rabbie Burns

An example of bowdlerisation in 'The National Song Book' is found in the version of 'A Man's A Man For A' That' by Burns. One of the five verses is left out. It is remarkable the song is included at all as it is a scathing critique of class inequality! It must have been too popular to leave out. But the verse that is left out is the one that is most explicit. (I have replaced a bowdlerised word with a lightly disguised four letter word)

Ye see yon birkie ca'd a lord
Wha struts an' stares an' a' that?
Though hundreds worship at his word
He's but a cunf for a' that
For a' that, an' a' that
His ribband, star, an' a' that
The man o' independent mind
He looks an' laughs at a' that

The description of the upper-class man as he who 'struts and stares' is perhaps the most brilliant concise class analysis I've ever read. But the suggestion that this eminent figure could (should!) be laughed at, must have been hard to stomach. Hence the omission of the verse.

Gordon Cox comments on the justification for the inclusion of Burns: "The inclusion of Jacobite songs in Stanford's National Song Book … [is] the celebration of a more turbulent past and is presented as a stage in the development towards a stable present." Cox, Towards the National Songbook, 1992

Cecil Sharp (1859–1924), the 'great folksong collector', was
furious about the bracketing together of the two categories folk and
national song. He maintained that the *National Song Book* list
contained 'scarcely a single genuine peasant-made folk song'
(School Music Review, June 1906: 1). He was to battle for a 'genuine'
folksong repertoire in schools for the next 20 years. It is perhaps
ironic that folksongs eventually became part of a rigid orthodoxy
that linked them inseparably with the values of national songs.

But everyone was agreed on the need to fight the pernicious effect
of popular culture such as music-hall songs and the need for the
nurturing of a nationalist identity with its ideas of racial purity.

*'The earliest form of music, folk-song, is essentially a communal
as well as a racial product. The natural musical idiom of a nation
will, therefore, be found in its purest and most unadulterated
form in its folk-music.'* Cecil Sharp in a pamphlet on **Folk Singing in
Schools** (c1913)

The aim is not to annihilate the working class but to simply empty
them of their culture! To remove any sense of self-worth or
cultural self determination and any developed independent
articulation of critical thought - Cultural annihilation!

Sharp versus Frank Kidson

- Cecil Sharp was a purist although still irrational from an ethnographic point of view! His passion had a powerful influence on the idea of what 'folk music' was - it wasn't urban, it didn't have an author, it had been passed down orally from time immemorial, etc.

- Sharp was taking a different route to the construction of a National Culture than Stanford. One he felt to be more pure.

- He did meet some resistance from the lower orders! **Frank Kidson (1855 - 1926)** showed that some 'old Welsh airs' lauded by Sharp were in fact English in origin (Kidson 1911). He was alert to the danger that Sharp's patriotism could lead to a warped and irrational account of history. In the end Sharp blocked the publication of Kidson and Moffat's book on the grounds of it being 'anti-harmonisation'.

"The social divide between Kidson and his contributors was much narrower than was the case with many collectors of the time and he appears to have treated them with respect and equality." Fivefingerfrank.co.uk

Free Education! - What's not to like?

- The collection, bowdlerisation and publication of rural culture led to the romantic construction of 'The Folk'. The weight of class condescension persuaded aspirational workers to accept this *re-branding*.

- Ideas of creating a national(ist) identity from above was intended to give a submissive and respectable working class a fitting national identity.

- This was to be achieved through the vehicle of education-for-all. Something working class leaders, like the Chartist William Lovett had been campaigning to achieve for decades.

From **1870** local authorities were enabled to set up schools where needed.

From **1880** compulsory elementary education was decreed.

The **1891** Elementary Education Act provided for the state payment of school fees up to ten shillings per head.

Finally, the **Education Act of 1918** abolished all fees for elementary schools.

NATIONALISM

NATIONALISM

School plus

From **1870** local authorities were enabled to set up schools where needed.

From **1880** compulsory elementary education was decreed.

The **1891** Elementary Education Act provided for the state payment of school fees up to ten shillings per head.

Finally, the **Education Act of 1918** abolished all fees for elementary schools.

Nationalism

CV Standford plus C Sharp

- A bowdlerised version of the collected and preserved old rural music culture, plus some popular patriotic favourites, was fed back to working-class children through the new state school system.

- This same material was used to create a national identity for people proud to unthinkingly serve The British Empire.

- The end result was that a people who constantly sung and whistled to themselves were hushed and made quiet. Like birds decimated by pollution.

1929

100 years
being our
rial along
thousands
ouses of pisé
all over
asing amount
s gone on
ay.
right shows
ther and her
front door of
welling in
the 1930s

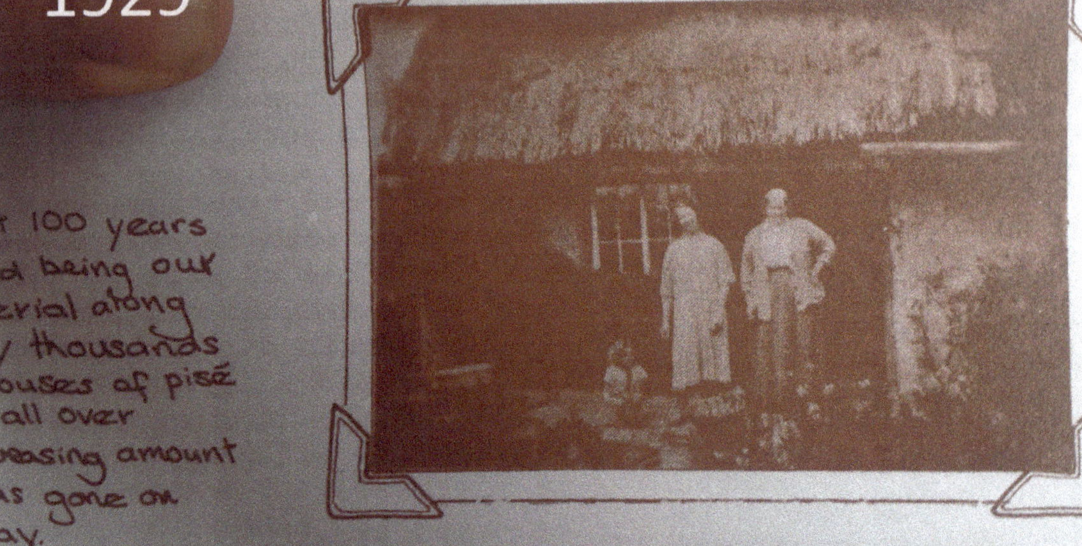

Why don't you hear anything these days about earth wall buildings?

Inasmuch as there is nothing in bare earth to <u>sell</u>, no commercial group can be found to extol its merits.

A page from my Survival Scrapbook 1972

- After two unbelievably horrific World Wars I was born in Hammersmith in London.

- Travelling back on steam trains to my mother's family in Nottingham - I saw Grandpa Sid's violin hung on the wall, but I *never heard it played*.

- My mum's family was royalist. Grandpa Sid stood up for the national anthem and during the Queen's speech on Xmas day. The 1953 Coronation was televised (There was one TV in the street!). We had 'our queen' in exchange for our loyalty and deference!

- No musical culture was passed on to me by my mother or father. Music was something you listened to on the radio and, from the mid Fifties, watched on TV.

- The only songs I vocalised were from the **BBC** schools **'Singing Together'** programmes that were a continuation of The National Songbook – with the same songs 50 years later!

- Within this bleak media landscape I intuitively looked out for my own heritage. The Skiffle craze brought us folk music from USA along with Trad Jazz. Lonnie Donegan was the skiffle star who reared into the broadcast media spotlight. His 1958 hit song *Tom Dooley* was not the respectable version of 'folk' culture that was generally broadcast.

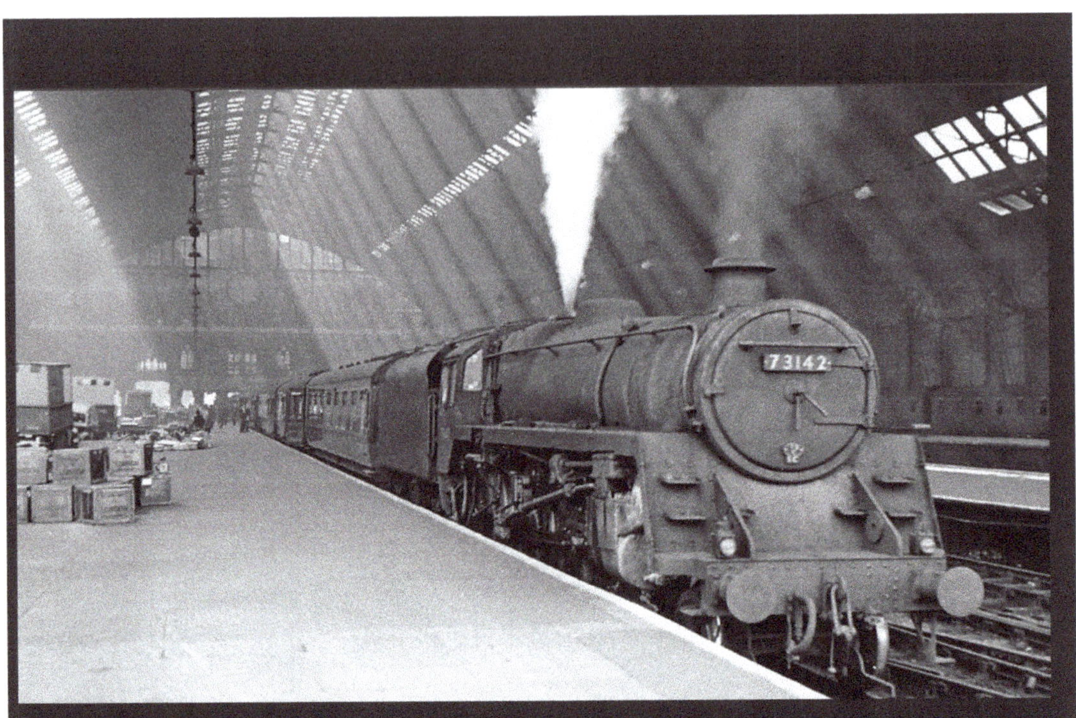

Leaving for Nottingham from
St Pancras Station in 1951

Photo by Ben Brooksbank 1957. A member of Geograph

Grandpa Sid's violin
in Nottingham was
hung on the wall -
but I **never heard it
played**.

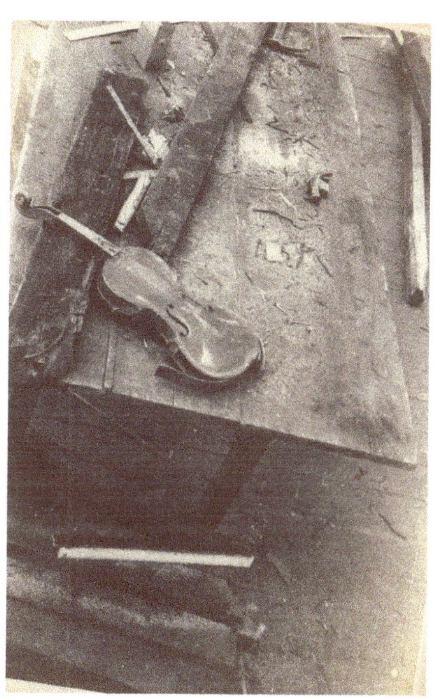

In 1892 my Grandma Daisy was born. She became one of ten children in rural Nottinghamshire / Lincolnshire. Her dad, Phillip Johnson, a primitive methodist preacher, died in 1902 when he was just 39 years old, leaving his wife, Maria, to raise the children alone. Daisy went away to work in service. First in Uppsley Castle in Yorkshire, where she rose to be a pastry cook, and then in a bourgeois town house in Nottingham. Around the time of the 1926 General Strike Sidney Smith, who was from a family of miners, had a fling with Daisy and they had a child; my mum Joan. At first they survived from two allotments. Sid sold the potatoes he grew from door to door. Later he got a lorry and started a mobile green grocery business. He played violin in a local chapel.

When I grew up I had NO KNOWLEDGE of a musical tradition from either side of my family. There was no music. We seemed to come from a place that just didn't have music!?

That seemed normal!

- And as if it wasn't enough to have this manufactured culture pumped into our heads through every school, there was the state monopoly of the new national broadcast media - BBC Radio!

- In the fifties they started broadcasting a programme called 'Singing Together' to schools. Schools no longer needed a compliant music teacher and piano in each school, they just needed a big radio set.

- What impressed me most were the beautifully illustrated booklets that accompanied each programme. At the end of the term we were allowed to take them home and keep them.

BBC radio - Singing Together

The only songs I vocalised in the Fifties were from the **BBC** schools **'Singing Together'** programmes - a continuation of The National Songbook – with the same songs 50 years later!

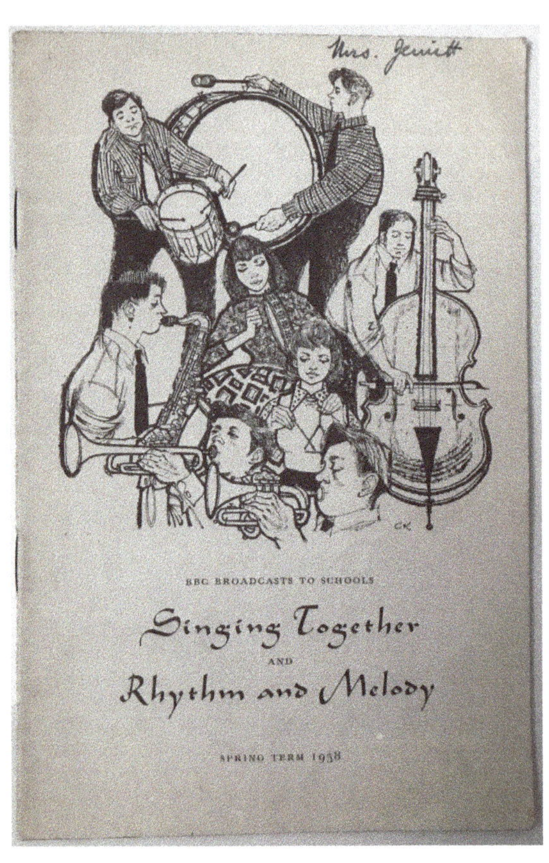

Drawing by Charles Keeping

My mother was aspirational, she wanted us to speak 'proper', not like those cockneys we lived amongst in Feltham. My mum dropped most of her Nottingham accent, and I could never get away with saying "ain't" or "fings" without a telling off. We did not seem to know any Midlands songs. We just didn't sing - apart from some nursery rhymes and lullabies. When I went to secondary school, we sang rude 'rugby songs' in the showers, where the tiling offered a nice reverb and we were separated from the delicate ears of the female sex!

As a family trying to move up in the world we just listened to the radio and thought that was it. We were grateful for having a laugh at The Goons or for listening to some bland dance band. After the horrors of the war we were 'happy' to consume culture quietly in the peaceful so-called 'lower middle-class' London suburbs. A PTSD kind of peace and quiet prevailed.

But out in the street it was different. The postman and the milkman whistled and sang if they felt the urge to. But sadly, they also gradually fell silent, as the message got through to them that singing in public was vulgar. Maybe down the pub when drunk but not to express 'joie de vivre' in the street. The upper class, with their haughty coldness gradually become the model for the social behaviour of ordinary people.

To Repeat! Working class culture was bowdlerised and fed back to working-class children in schools from the 1900s through the 1970s. At home many of our parents were no longer singing. What this extraordinarily malevolent trick achieved, over a period of fifty years of state schooling, was to persuade a large section of the 'respectable' working class that they had no live culture of any value. What survived was too vulgar or shallow and should be disowned if you aspired to be an educated person, rather than a person who was 'common as muck'. The only type of culture worth aspiring to was serious music - ideally classical music. Radio, and then TV, was the voice of the state carrying this hurtful message directly into the heart of every home.

BOwDlerisation

British *possessions* in 1915

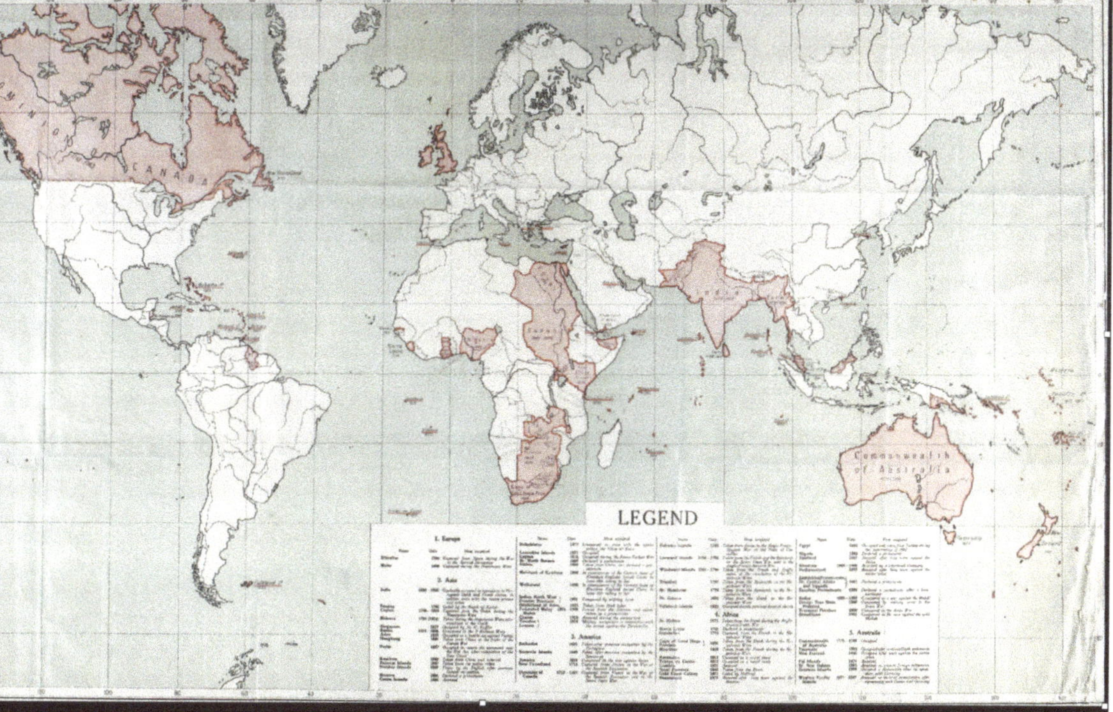

The background to this story

The end result was that
a people who had sung
whistled to them-
selves daily for millennia
were gradually hushed
made quiet through the
like birds choked
and silenced by pollution.
People were silenced by
this **cultural oppression.**

Oppression can be defined as…

- The systematic devaluation and hurting of one social group or class by another that sees itself as superior.

- Negative self-images are internalised. E.g. so that working-class people themselves come to believe they are not cut-out to be intellectuals or artists. I.e. the creators of culture.

- This internalised oppression has to be renewed for every generation to maintain the illusion that one group of people is superior to, and more intelligent than, another. +

A definition of culture

- 'The idea of culture is a general reaction to a general and major change in the conditions of our common life. Its basic element is its effort at *total qualitative assessment* ... What it indicates is a process not a conclusion.'

  (Raymond Williams, 1958, p285)

- This modern, inclusive concept of culture developed in the wake of the egalitarian and inclusive concept of democracy that was set alight in Europe by the

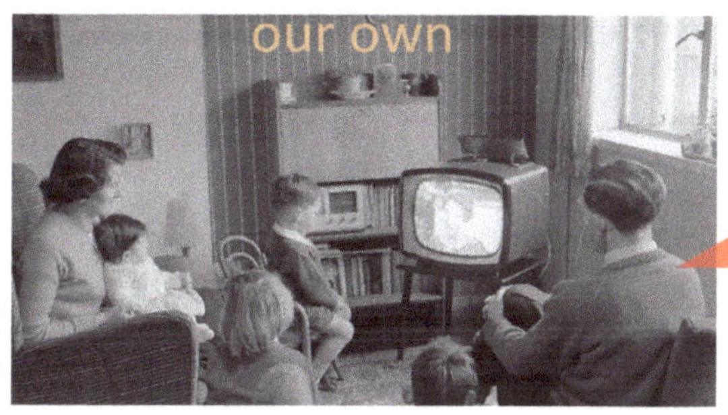

When I grew up I had NO KNOWLEDGE of a musical
tradition from either side of my family. There was
no singing, no music, no dance. We seemed to
come from a place that just didn't produce music!?
*A strange idea – humans who don't sing! Or
humans without a culture!? 1950s*

Aspiration for upward mobility

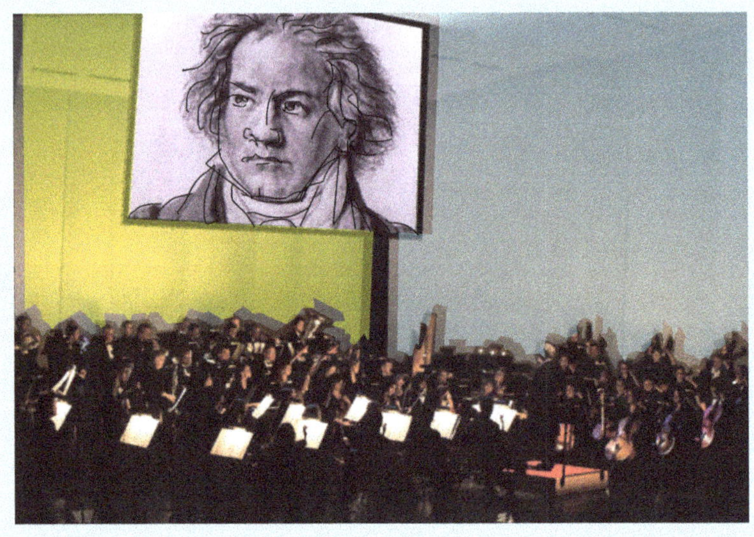

Classical music - Beethoven's 5th on brittle 78rpm records+

- **We had a set of 78s of** Beethoven's 5th **which came with our radiogram as a hand-me-down from better-off neighbours. My mother said this was** the music to listen to - but she didn't! **The records got one play and were then left on the shelf.**

- **The myth about pop culture was that its vinyl 45s** wouldn't pass the test of time. **They were a waste of money and our time.** (Adorno agreed)

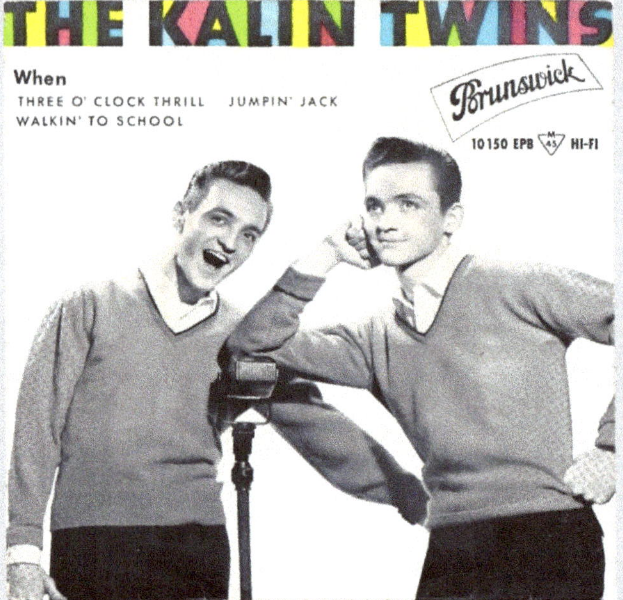

1958 Vulgarity ! Subversive B-sides

Did they really sing "Oh yeah! Do you want a bunk up?"!!?

- George Reptowski who lived in Brixton called me up on our new telephone. He was excited about the new record he wanted to play me when my family visited his family who lived on Burton Road in Brixton.

- This record apparently had 'dirty words' on the B-side that the record publishers hadn't noticed! A sensational break in the all pervasive control of popular music.

- George Reptowski who lived in Brixton called me up on our new telephone. He was excited about the new record he had to play me when my family visited him on Sunday.

- This record had 'dirty words' on the B side that the record

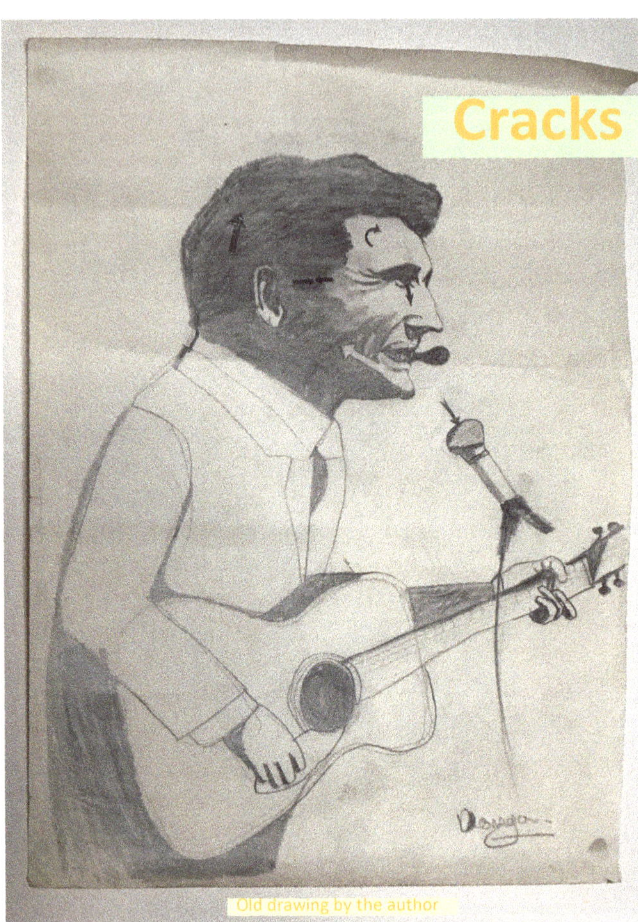

Old drawing by the author

- **Class deference** was embodied in the spectacle of 'our' Queen.

- So in 1960 when Lonnie Donegan performed musichall style comedy ditty 'My Old Man's a Dustman' direct to the Queen at the Royal Variety Show on ATV, my internalised deference evaporated!

- It was five years later that the next crack in the spectacle occurred (for me). A rock group, **The Who,** appeared on ***Ready Steady Go!*** a programme put together by Elkan Allan and hosted by the top Mod, Kathy McGowen. Their song was a sensational blast of anger and noise, straight into my (mother's) pristine living.

The Screen shatters 1965

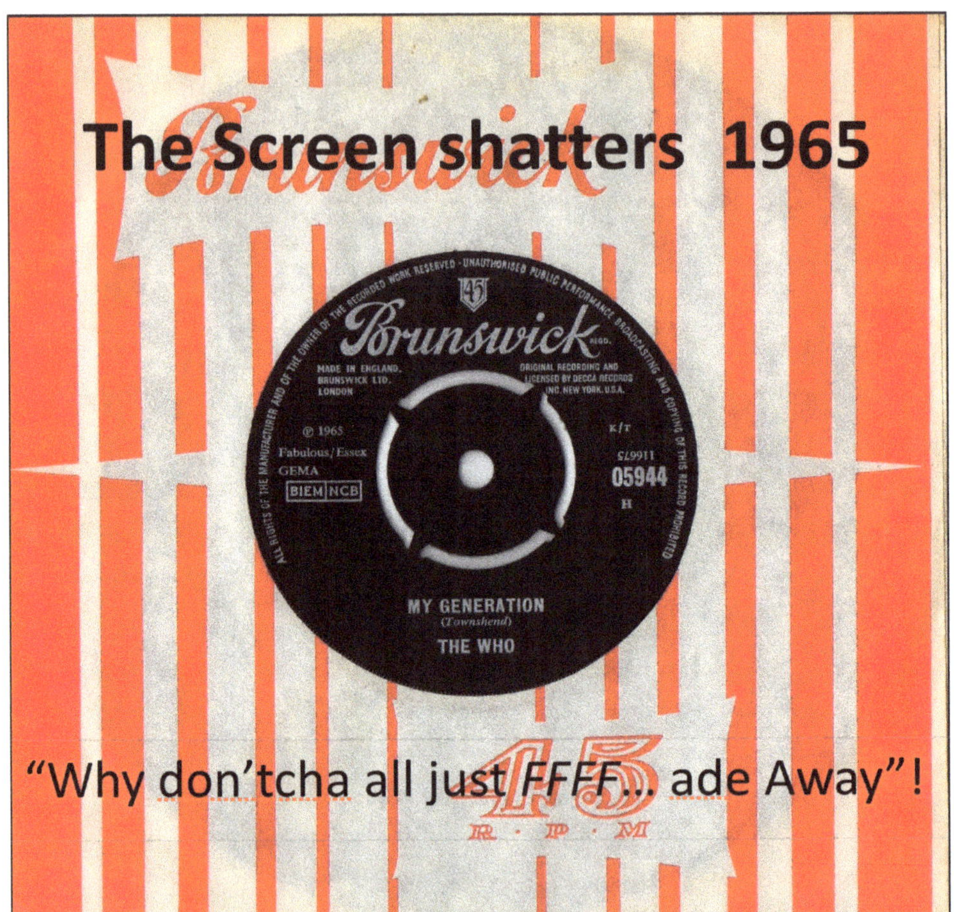

"Why don'tcha all just *FFFF*... ade Away"!

This kinda raw rock music owed everything to the American blues! And it was about the same time that the legendary Sonny Boy Williamson II came to Chertsey! Just a few miles from our suburban house. Wow!

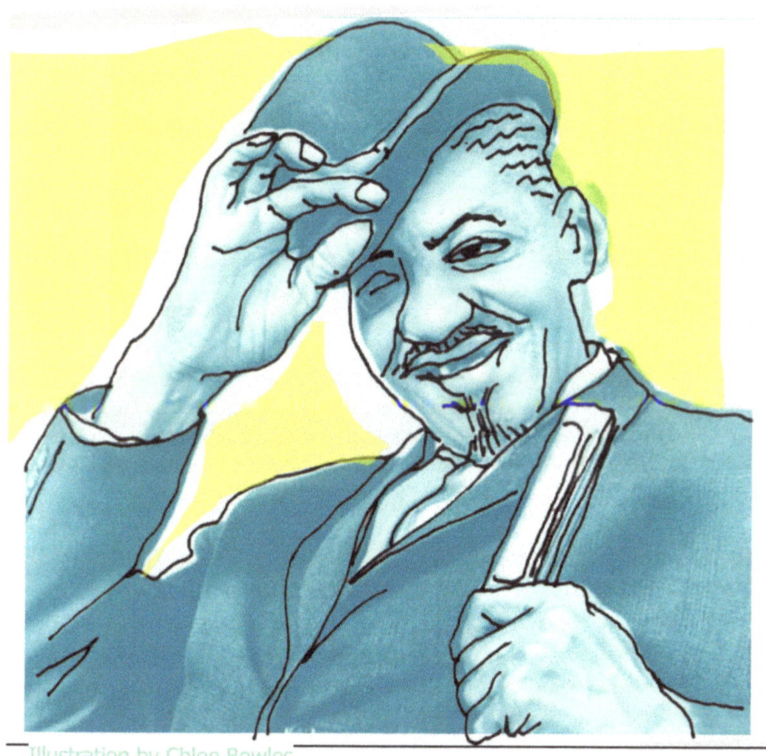

Illustration by Chloe Bowles

This is my memory of hearing The Cream in the Ricky Tick club in Windsor c1966

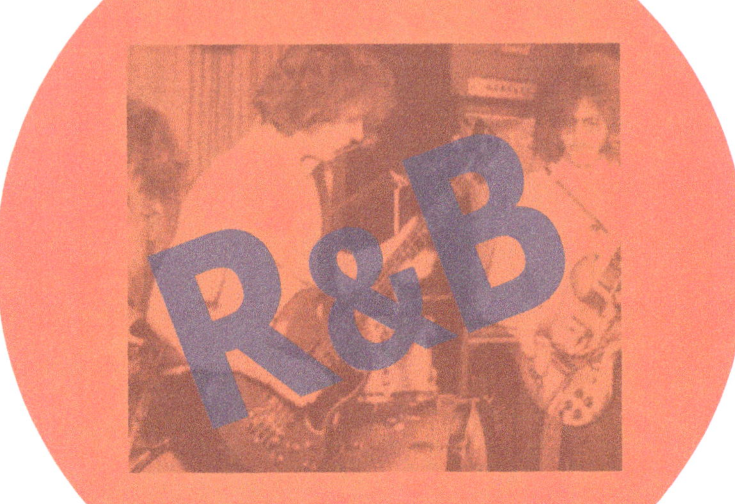

- Seeing Eric Clapton play his guitar in that tiny club made me realise that working-class culture was the equal of any 'classical' music in terms of sheer virtuosity and the beauty and aesthetic complexity of musical relations and emotive power that it could generate. It was an emotional moment!

- The myth of the inferiority of working-class culture exploded in my face.

- Things were now moving fast and I was to leave home at the end of 1966 and go to Portsmouth Polytechnic.

Suddenly I was a hippy and the world started revolting big time. This is the song that 'blew my mind' when I heard it in a seedy bedsit in Portsmouth 1967 /8

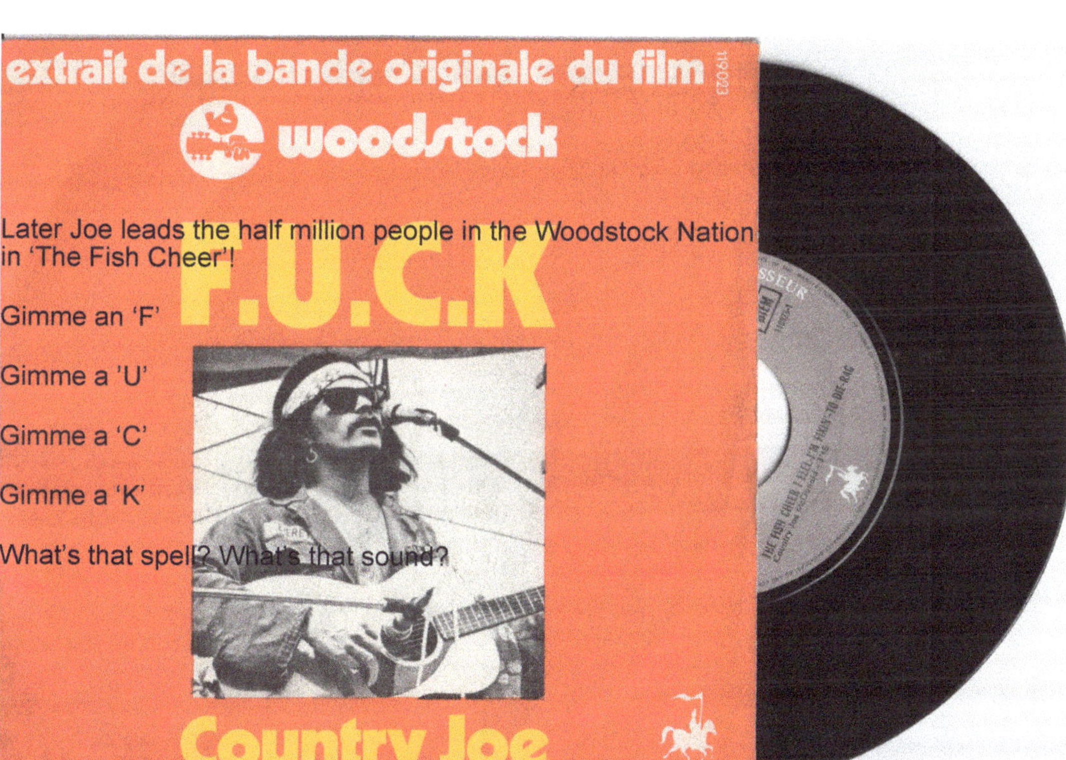

Then from this heady mix of African-American voices from the past (often heard live, loud, intimate) and the virtuosity of the upstart Eric Clapton and the profanity of Country Joe .... I stepped into a darkened room in The Place, near Euston, and found myself.

The group I went to see was the **AMM**. Maybe John Stevens of the Spontaneous Music Ensemble had recommended them, or maybe it was a review in the International Times - I can't remember. Anyway there I was and the room erupted in the most extraordinary cacaphony of sub-musical sounds. Then the roar of noise settled, gradually, into some delicate whisps of electronic noise - a crackling radio burst in which was a fragment of the global reality. Soon the roar swept back through the room again and this time it swept me off my feet into a liberated zone.

Liberated from conventions and stiff traditions into a world of new beginnings. It was raw noise and yet it was ordered by an intelligent sensibility and the combination of sounds I was familiar with.

AMM was a closed group of skilled musician improvisers but I was invited by Cornelius Cardew, one of the musicians, to join a new thing he was organising: The Scratch Orchestra which was to be open to contributions of sound and performance from 'everyone'. The Scratch Orchestra was defined as: 'A large number of enthusiasts pooling their resources (not primarily material resources) and assembling for action...' My time in The Scratch Orchestra lasted from 1969 to 1972 and gave me the most powerful and xtra-ordinary opportunities.

I've written about this in another book in which I attempt to suggest why this collective improvisation is relevant to the re-invention of working-class culture.

A Scratch Orchestra: draft constitution

Cornelius Cardew

Definition: A Scratch Orchestra is a large number of enthusiasts pooling their resources (not primarily material resources) and assembling for action (music-making, performance, edification).

Note: The word music and its derivatives are here not understood to refer exclusively to sound and related phenomena (hearing, *etc*). What they do refer to is flexible and depends entirely on the members of the Scratch Orchestra.

The Scratch Orchestra intends to function in the public sphere, and this function will be expressed in the form of—for lack of a better word—concerts. In rotation (starting with the youngest) each member will have the option of designing a concert. If the option is taken up, all details of that concert are in the hands of that person or his delegates; if the option is waived the details of the concert will be determined by random methods, or by voting (a vote determines which of these two). The material of these concerts may be drawn, in part or wholly, from the basic repertory categories outlined below.

1 Scratch music

Each member of the orchestra provides himself with a notebook (or Scratchbook) in which he notates a number of accompaniments, performable continuously for indefinite periods. The number of accompaniments in each book should be equal to or greater than the current number of members of the orchestra. An accompaniment is defined as music that allows a solo (in the event of one occurring) to be appreciated as such. The notation may be accomplished using any means—verbal, graphic, musical, collage, *etc*—and should be regarded as a period of training: never notate more than one accompaniment in a day. If many ideas arise on one day they may all be incorporated in one accompaniment. The last accompaniment in the list has the status of a solo and if used should only be used as such. On the addition of further items, what was previously a solo is relegated to the status of an accompaniment, so that at any time each player has only one solo and that his most recent. The sole differentiation between a solo and an accompaniment is in the mode of playing.

The performance of this music can be entitled *Scratch Overture*, *Scratch Interlude* or *Scratch Finale* depending on its position in the concert.

2 Popular Classics

Only such works as are familiar to several members are eligible for this category. Particles of the selected works will be gathered in Appendix 1. A particle could be: a page of score, a page or more of the part for one instrument or voice, a page of an arrangement, a thematic analysis, a gramophone record, *etc*.

The technique of performance is as follows: a qualified member plays the given particle, while the remaining players join in as best they can, playing along, contributing whatever they can recall of the work in question, filling the gaps of memory with improvised variational material.

The Musical Times, Vol. 110, No. 1516, 125th Anniversary Issue. (Jun., 1969), pp. 617+619

As is appropriate to the classics, avoid losing touch with the reading player (who may terminate the piece at his discretion), and strive to act concertedly rather than independently. These works should be programmed under their original titles.

3 Improvisation Rites

A selection of the rites in *Nature Study Notes* will be available in Appendix 2. Members should constantly bear in mind the possibility of contributing new rites. An improvisation rite is not a musical composition; it does not attempt to influence the music that will be played; at most it may establish a community of feeling, or a communal starting-point, through ritual. Any suggested rite will be given a trial run and thereafter left to look after itself. Successful rites may well take on aspects of folklore, acquire nicknames, *etc*.

Free improvisation may also be indulged in from time to time.

4 Compositions

Appendix 3 will contain a list of compositions performable by the orchestra. Any composition submitted by a member of the orchestra will be given a trial run in which all terms of the composition will be adhered to as closely as possible. Unless emphatically rejected, such compositions will probably remain as compositions in Appendix 3. If such a composition is repeatedly acclaimed it may qualify for inclusion in the Popular Classics, where it would be represented by a particle only, and adherence to the original terms of the composition would be waived.

5 Research Project

A fifth repertory category may be evolved through the Research Project, an activity obligatory for all members of the Scratch Orchestra, to ensure its cultural expansion.

The Research Project. The universe is regarded from the viewpoint of travel. This means that an infinite number of research vectors are regarded as hypothetically travellable. Travels may be undertaken in many dimensions, *eg* temporal, spatial, intellectual, spiritual, emotional. I imagine any vector will be found to impinge on all these dimensions at some point or other. For instance, if your research vector is the *Tiger*, you could be involved in time (since the tiger represents an evolving species), space (a trip to the zoo), intellect (the tiger's biology), spirit (the symbolic values acquired by the tiger) and emotion (your subjective relation to the animal).

The above is an intellectual structure, so for a start let's make the research vector a word or group of words rather than an object or an impression *etc*. A record of research is kept in the Scratchbook and this record may be made available to all.

From time to time a journey will be proposed (Journey to Mars, Journey to the Court of Wu Ti, Journey to the Unconscious, Journey to West Ham, *etc*). A discussion will suffice to provide a rough itinerary (*eg* embarkation at Cape Kennedy, type of vehicle to be used, number of hours in space, choice of a landing site, return to earth or not, *etc*).

Members whose vectors are relevant to this journey can pursue the relevance and consider the musical application of their research; members whose vectors are irrelevant (research on rocket fuels won't help with a journey to the Court of Wu Ti) can put themselves at the disposal of the others for the musical realization of their research.

A date can be fixed for the journey, which will take the form of a performance.

Conduct of research. Research should be through direct experience rather than academic; neglect no channels. The aim is: by direct contact, imagination, identification and study to get as close as possible to the object of your research. Avoid the mechanical accumulation of data; be constantly awake to the possibility of inventing new research techniques. The record in the Scratchbook should be a record of your activity rather than an accumulation of data. That means: the results of your research are in you, not in the book.

Example

Research vector	Research record
The Sun	29.vi. Looked up astronomical data in *EB* & made notes to the accpt of dustmotes (symbol of *EB*) and sunbeams
	1-28. viii. Holiday in the Bahamas to expose myself to the sun.
	29.vii. Saw 'the Sun' as a collection of 6 letters and wrote out the 720 combinations of them.
	1.viii. Got interested in Sun's m. or f. gender in different languages, and thence to historical personages regarded as the Sun (like Mao Tse-tung). Sought an astrological link between them.
Astrology	3.viii. Had my horoscope cast by Mme Jonesky of Gee's Court. *etc*

(note that several vectors can run together)
(the facing page should be left blank for notes on eventual musical realizations)

Spare time activity for orchestra members: each member should work on the construction of a unique mechanical, musical, electronic or other instrument.

APPENDICES

Appendix 1 *Popular Classics*
Particles from: Beethoven, *Pastoral Symphony*
Mozart, *Eine Kleine Nachtmusik*
Rachmaninov, *Second Piano Concerto*
J. S. Bach, *Sheep may safely graze*
Cage, *Piano Concert*
Brahms, *Requiem*
Schoenberg, *Pierrot Lunaire*
etc
(blank pages for additions)

Appendix 2 *Improvisation Rites from the book 'Nature Study Notes'* (two examples must suffice)
1 Initiation of the pulse
Continuation of the pulse
Deviation by means of accentuation, decoration, contradiction
HOWARD SKEMPTON

14 All seated loosely in a circle, each player shall write or draw on each of the ten fingernails of the player on his left.
No action or sound is to be made by a player after his fingernails have received this writing or drawing, other than music.
Closing rite: each player shall erase the marks from the fingernails of another player. Your participation in the music ceases when the marks have been erased from your fingernails.
(Groups of two or more late-comers may use the same rite to join in an improvisation that is already in progress.)
(blank pages for additions)   RICHARD REASON

Appendix 3 *List of compositions*
Lamonte Young, *Poem*
Von Biel, *World II*
Terry Riley, *in C*
Christopher Hobbs, *Voicepiece*
Stockhausen, *Aus den Sieben Tagen*
Wolff, *Play*
Cage, *Variations VI*
etc
(blank pages for additions)

Appendix 4 *Special Projects and supplementary material*
(blank pages)

At time of going to press, the orchestra has 60 members. More are welcome. A meeting to confirm draft constitution and initiate training should precede the summer recess. Projected inaugural concert: November 1969. Interested parties should write to Cornelius Cardew, 112 Elm Grove Road, London SW13.

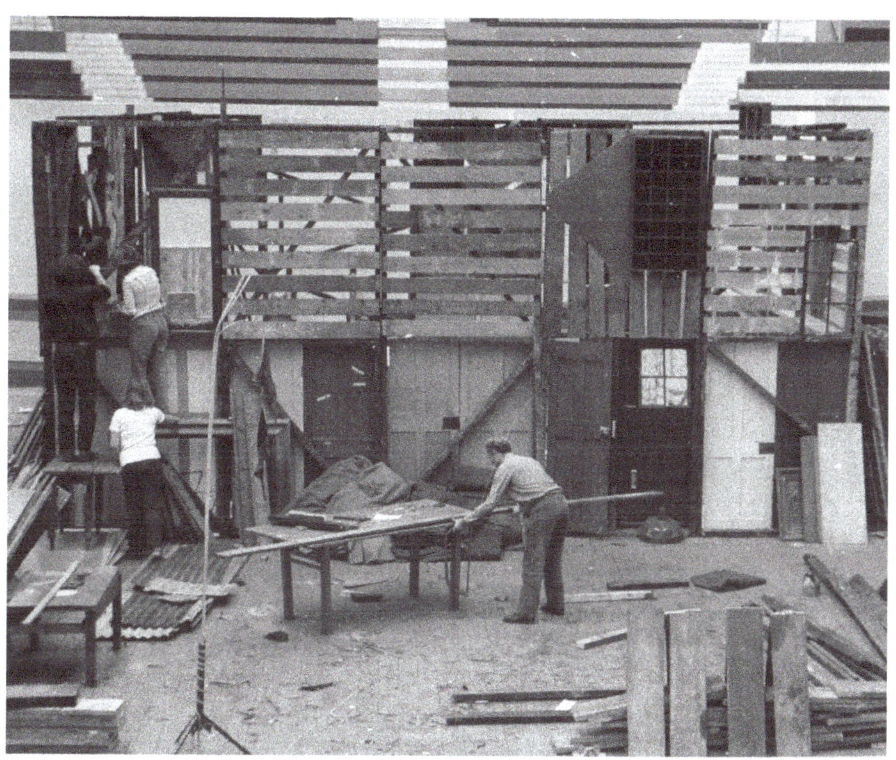

Possibly my main contribution to the Scratch Orchestra activity was 'The Scratch Cottage'. Seen here under construction by members of the orchestra. It was shown in the 'Art Spectrum' exhibition in Alexandra Palace, 1972 and was intended to house *The Refuse Collection* (the conventional artworks of orchestra members... now redundant - an idea by Tim Mitchel)   Photo by the author.

The interesting thing for me about Christopher Small's 1998 book 'Musicking' was it's analysis of classical music that revealed its class operation. **The first** bourgeois literary idea about music is that music's essential spirit is captured by a *written score*. The next step is that this score is printed and published to claim the originality of its singular authorship. **The second** idea is that when this composition is performed, it is a one-way communication from composer to audience, usually through the medium of an orchestra. Neither the audience nor the musician should contribute meaning, although they are allowed a modicum of interpretation. **The third** idea is that there is little or no feedback from the audience, nor communication between the audience, whilst the performance is in progress - silent listening and stillness of body are required. **Fourth,** the score sets the upper limit of what can be achieved. **Fifth**, the quality of serious musical works is autonomous of context - and so assumed to be universally valid. (P.6)

These parameters are set to place 'classical' or 'serious' music above the rest of the music in the world what Small calls, *"The great restless ocean of human musicking"* that does not rely on written notation. For Small this 'ocean' of sound is most commonly an encounter between human beings, in a particular setting, in which sounds play a central organising role. He calls this process musicking.

He deconstructs the symphony concert as an example. It has now become global and aspirational: a central musical rite of the new bourgeois classes as capitalist production spread around the globe. Small seeks to find the meaning of the concert in the relationships between the people who make and attend this event rather that the relationships of notes in the score. He notes the growth of prestige concert halls around the world in the second half of the C20th. To have a concert hall is a civic essential *"to signal entry into the developed world"*. There are perhaps as many recently-built concert halls as ones that date from when most of the music was composed in the previous century.

"A grand, ceremonial space such as this imposes a mode of behaviour on those who are unaccustomed to it. The (audience) become somewhat self-conscious, lowering their voices, muting their gestures, looking around them, bearing themselves in general more

formally. They may even feel something like awe." p.23
"What the (concert halls) all have in common is, first, that they convey an impression of opulence, even sumptuousness. There is wealth here, and the power that wealth brings ... Second, they allow no communication with the outside world. Performers and listeners alike are isolated here from the world of their everyday lives." p.25
 "The auditoriums design not only discourages communication amongst members of the audience but it also tells them they are there to listen and not talk back." p.27

The social contact between audience and players is reduced with separate exits and the realised platform. He contrasts this separation of functions with the old 'Pleasure Gardens' of London. (e.g. Vauxhall Pleasure Gardens) in which the social classes mingled and there was greater access for the local artist. The concert experience is that of passive and elite consumption. We can see it as a submission of the regular audience to bourgeois relations. Another small avant-garde scene is reserved for experimentalism and critique - a scene that Small does not seem to know or consider.

The conservative canon is extended in a sophisticated way into the playlist of BBC Radio 3 and, in a banal way, to Classic Fm. Works by great experimental composers of the C20th like John Cage or Cornelius Cardew, are rarely heard on Radio Three. Small does not extend his argument to the avant-garde.

The logistics and infrastructure of a modern performance are very far from spontaneous. There is a vast management structure that promotes and defends the exclusive nature to the art form. Performers can only take part if they make their way 'up' through layers of competitions that serve to exclude most musicians. The professionals who do not make it through this highly-selective process are left with less lucrative markets and are lucky if they get a season's work in a London musical. There is no place for amateurs except in a few Youth Orchestras.

The repertory that attracts a profitable audience is frozen in period before the first decades of the C20th. A finite number of classic works to be shared out further restricts the programme. The effect of all this is a high culture that can challenge or relate to nothing in our contemporary experience. It simply celebrates a formative moment of maturation in European bourgeois class and the ritualised gathering of a thousand or more bourgeois persons at such an event, is simply a ritual self-affirmation of their superior status.

"In the improvising orchestras of the first brilliant explosion of opera in the early seventeenth century, it was leadership rather than conducting that was the keynote" p.82. "To hear a symphony orchestra play, in fact, is to be presented with the very image of power that is under control and harnessed to a purpose" p.122.

It creates in cultural form the image of industrial production with its core myth that it is the bourgeois who are the creators (composers) and the proletarians merely trained bodies who rigorously follow the score of the masters.

"Art galleries are ritual buildings as much as are concert halls and theatres and as much as are churches and temples" p.108.

Behaviour and passivity of consumption is circumscribed in a similar way but at least the works of art might relate to the time in which we live. In spite of this the canon of classical music is promoted (it would seem quaint if it was not delivered with such authority) as the only real or serious music. If you are not proficient as a performer or knowledgeable as a consumer of classical music, you are not 'musical'. If you like vulgar forms of music you have inferior taste or 'no' taste.

"The voice is at the centre of all musical activity, but it is all too easy to silence and very hard to reactivate, since those who have been silenced in this way have been wounded in a very intimate and crucial part of their being" p.212

"… now that Albertine had gone out, I went and took my stand for a moment at the window. There was at first a silence, amid which the whistle of the tripe vendor and the horn of the tramcar made the air ring in different octaves, like a blind piano-tuner. Then gradually the interwoven motives became distinct, and others were combined with them. There was also a new whistle, the call of a vendor, the nature of whose wares I have never discovered, a whistle that was itself exactly like the scream of the tramway and, as it was not carried out of earshot by its own velocity, one thought of a single car, not endowed with motion, or broken down, immobilised, screaming at short intervals like a dying animal. And I felt that, should I ever have to leave this aristocratic quarter — unless it were to move to one that was entirely plebeian — the streets and boulevards of central Paris (where the fruit, fish and other trades stabilised in huge stores, rendered superfluous the cries of the street hawkers, who for that matter would not have been able to make themselves heard) would seem to me very dreary, quite uninhabitable, stripped, drained of all these litanies of the small trades and peripatetic victuals, deprived of the orchestra that returned every morning to charm me …

The throb of a violin was due at one time to the passing of a motor-car, at another to my not having put enough water in my electric kettle. In the middle of the symphony there rang out an old-fashioned 'air'; replacing the sweet seller, who generally accompanied her song with a rattle, the toy seller, to whose pipe was attached a jumping jack which he sent flying in all directions, paraded similar puppets for sale, and without heeding the ritual declamation of Gregory the Great, the reformed declamation of Palestrina or the lyrical declamation of the modern composers, intoned at the top of his voice, a belated adherent of pure melody."

Excerpt From Marcel Proust's 'The Captive', p.121 Translation by Carol Clark

From the end of **The Scratch Orchestra,** I headed away from music and wrote and published books, and became a visual artist for three decades. Then I came back to music in 2008 with the idea of **'Agit Disco'**. It had been in the back of my mind for a long time but it was finally realised as a series of CD length playlists of 'music that had had a political effect on your life'. The people putting together each playlist were called the *selectors*. The idea was to highlight the working-class music that had been made invisible by the processes of repression and exclusion that I have discussed above.

One of the ways we can begin to repair working-class musical culture is to collect and promote our own class-conscious selections of music. An example of someone on my playlist was the singer songwriter Steve Cope who lived in my area of South London. He wrote and sang songs with the most riveting lyrics and published them as a cassette that sold locally through the **56a Infoshop** (see illustration opposite) But he was pretty much assured of no further exposure due to the political lyrics of his songs, along with his own uncompromising anti-commercial stance.

Obviously this is not the only way that musics are made less visible to a wider public, sometimes it is just a matter of a relative lack of airplay. Anyway, in 2012 a book of 23 of these playlists was published by **Mute Books** and in 2018 an expanded Japanese edition was published by **ele king books** (sic). An updated Agit Disco ebook, with links to most of the music, is published simultaneously with this edition. Search - ISBN 978-1-870736-20-6

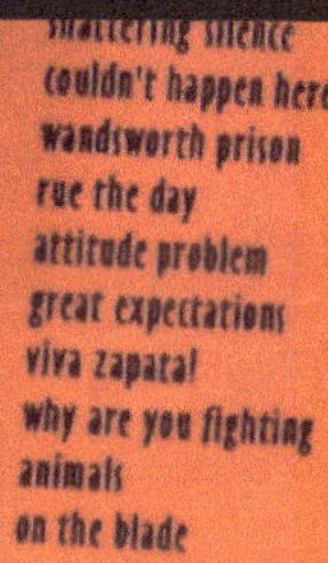

shattering silence
couldn't happen here
wandsworth prison
rue the day
attitude problem
great expectations
viva zapata!
why are you fighting
animals
on the blade

the 1926 committee were
clare clark flute &
percussion
marcos s ramos
percussion
dave murrell bass,
keyboards & percussion
steve cope vocals,
guitar, harmonica,
percussion & banjo
all songs written by
steve cope
arrangements by the
1926 committee

more of the same

the 1926 committee

more of the same
the 1926 committee

Agit Disco

- One of the things to disappear from the nation's media screens in the process of bowdlerisation is the **politics** in music. This includes the stories of how music takes part in our political unfolding, revealing truths about the world or supporting us in our struggles against oppression. This is a concept wider than 'protest music'.

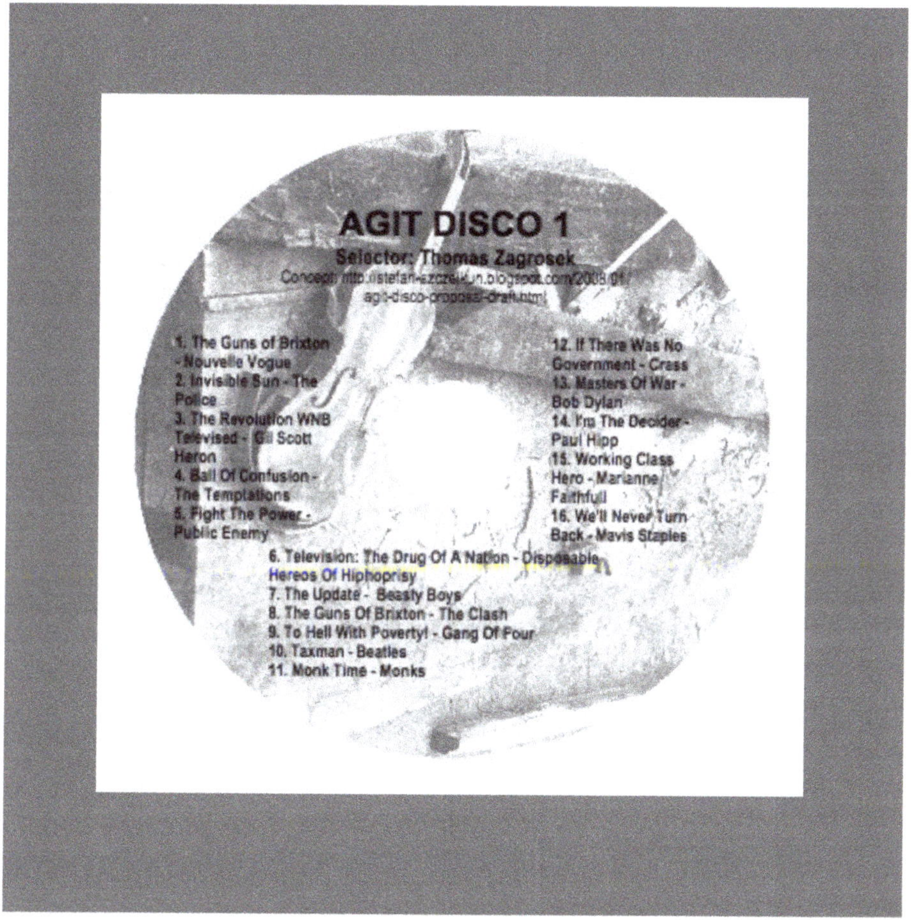

AGIT DISCO 1

Selector: Thomas Zagrosek

Concept: http://stefan-szczelkun.blogspot.com/2008/01/
agit-disco-proposal-draft.html

1. The Guns of Brixton - Nouvelle Vogue
2. Invisible Sun - The Police
3. The Revolution WNB Televised - Gil Scott Heron
4. Ball Of Confusion - The Temptations
5. Fight The Power - Public Enemy
6. Television: The Drug Of A Nation - Disposable Hereos Of Hiphoprisy
7. The Update - Beasty Boys
8. The Guns Of Brixton - The Clash
9. To Hell With Poverty! - Gang Of Four
10. Taxman - Beatles
11. Monk Time - Monks
12. If There Was No Government - Crass
13. Masters Of War - Bob Dylan
14. I'm The Decider - Paul Hipp
15. Working Class Hero - Marianne Faithfull
16. We'll Never Turn Back - Mavis Staples

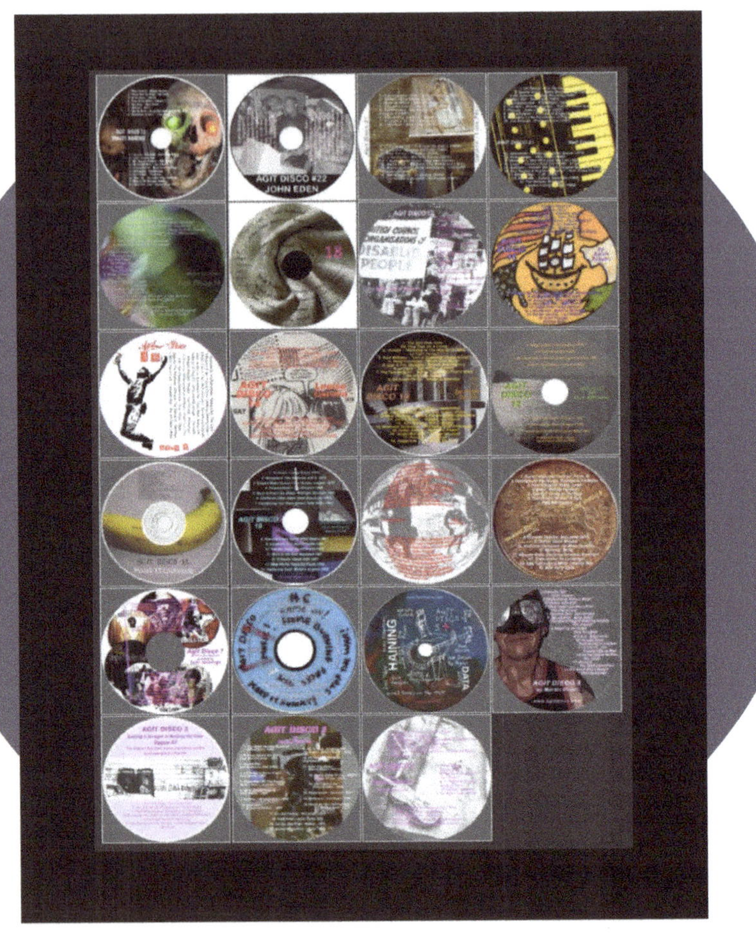
AGIT DISCO #22
JOHN EDEN
DISABLED PEOPLE
AGIT DISCO
HAINING
DATA
AGIT DISCO 3
AGIT DISCO

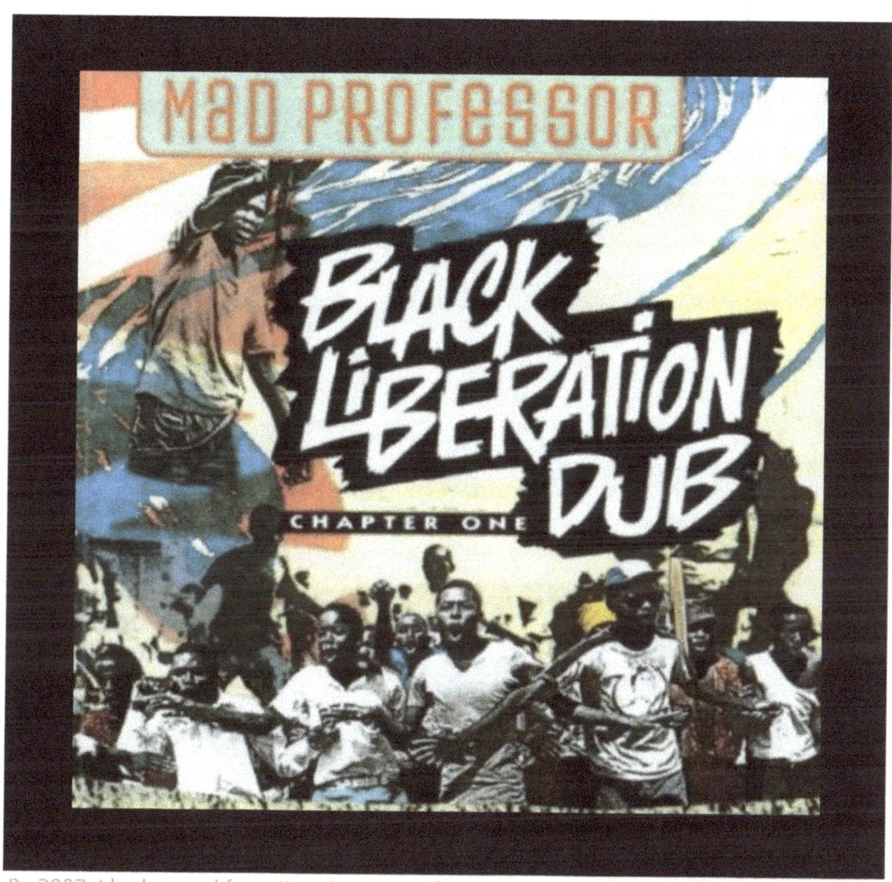

By 2007, I had moved from Kennington to Thornton Heath. The Mad Professor a famous local record producer was doing his own 'agitdisco' project.

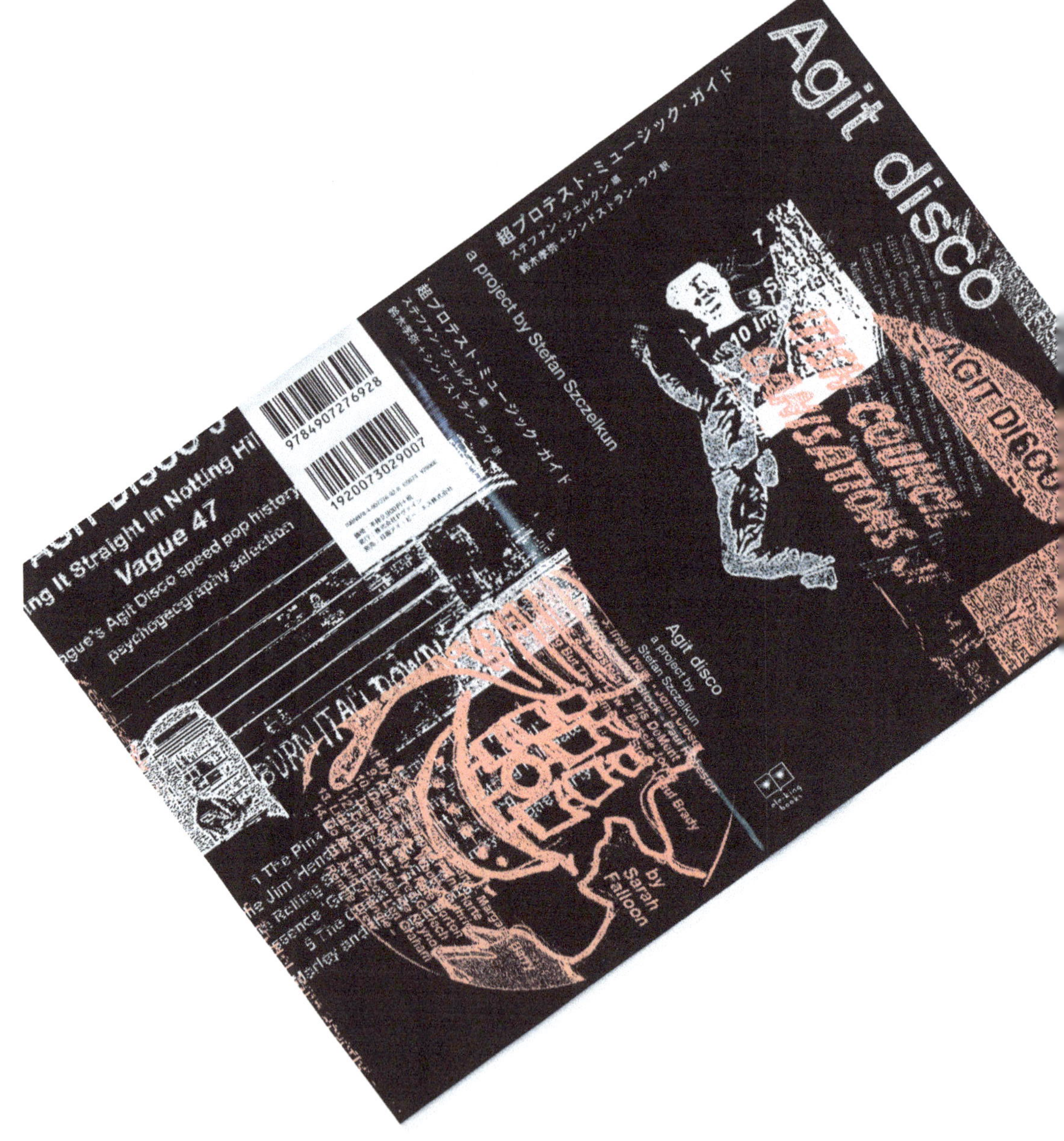

Agit disco
超プロテスト・ミュージック・ガイド
ステファン・シェルクン編
鈴木孝弥＋シンドストラン・ラヴ訳
a project by Stefan Szczelkun
AGIT DISCO
COMPILATIONS
Agit disco
a project by
Stefan Szczelkun
by
Sarah Falloon
elektron books
9784907276928
1920073029007
Vague 47
Vague's Agit Disco speed pop history
psychogeography selection
Straight In Notting Hill

Summary of Argument

The working-class have been subject to a kind of cultural imperialism which entails the culture of the ruling class being imposed as a condition of 'aspiration'. The culture of subaltern peoples is ruled as invalid. The bourgeois groups, that have power in society, control how the rest of the population interpret the world, communicate and play in crucial areas.

"The institution of slavery usually tried to deny its victims their native cultural identity. Torn out of their own cultural milieus, they were expected to abandon their heritage and to adopt at least part of their enslavers' culture." Encyclopaedia Britannica (online, accessed 24-12-18)

The global shift of peoples from a rural existence to life in a town or city led to a scramble by the ruling classes to re-establish control. In Britain this happened almost unchallenged between 1800 and 1950, but globally we may assume it is an ongoing process. The bourgeoisie were successful containing this 'cultural revolution' in Britain by using the power of education and media, which they had fashioned in the image of their own values.

"Culture, far from being democratically created by the countless interactions of the population as a whole (sort of like Adam Smith's mythical market place composed of innumerable buyers and sellers), is overwhelmingly shaped and manipulated by the ruling class in ways favourable to its continued rule and people seeing that rule as legitimate, natural, and inevitable." L. Richard Della Fave reviewing Ratner 2011)

Della Fave is talking about the dominant culture, the European model that is still being used to globalise cultural practises and discourse. Oral cultures and languages are exactly made from innumerable interactions and presentations of statements that are taken up, or ignored or modified.

Silencing may be a part of all oppression.

It would make sense, as a rising against oppression requires us to be articulate and communicate well with each other. It has been said that silencing is central to women's history. A quick search produced the following quotes:

"Silence and shame are contagious; so are courage and speech. Even now, when women begin to speak of their experience, others step forward to bolster the earlier speaker and to share their own experience. A brick is knocked loose, another one; a dam breaks, the waters rush forth." Rebecca Solnit, The Mother of All Questions, Harpers Magazine, October 2015

Whilst oppression still dominates our societies globally, any efforts we seem to make to rationally decide that inequality is 'bad' or wrong will be thwarted by the insidious nature of embedded myths of who has the right to speak. Michele George points out, in the context of affluent Western societies, 'not singing' is the norm. She states: "To not sing is entirely socially acceptable ... It's not like a social stigma" Michele George, quoted in Victoria Moon Joyce, 2003:

"Even though I sang all the time, I was aware that I couldn't burst out in song whenever I wanted to. I noticed that most people didn't sing. On trips when I sang in the car, I would notice the radio would get turned on automatically ... I learned that most of the world was a 'no singing zone' - the only time I heard people sing to each other in public was either in bars or singing "Happy Birthday," usually with some degree of embarrassment. Susan Hale, 'Song and Silence: voicing the soul' 1995.

"The more I study this phenomenon of anxious singers or so-called non-singers, the more I am convinced that it's really a product of white, bourgeois respectability and a quest for perfection – unattainable cultural expectations that keep everyone nervous, self-policing and anxious about fitting in. If you're wondering what white space looks like, look around - because we're in it." Victoria Moon Joyce, 'Turn Off the Radio and Sing for Your Lives', from Karen Warren's 'Women's Voices in Experiential Education' 1996.

"According to Freire, oppressed people become so powerless that they do not even talk about their oppression. If they reach this stage of oppression, it creates a culture wherein it is forbidden to even mention the injustices that are being committed. The oppressed are silenced. They have no voice and no will."
adapted from Iris Young,
'Oppression, Privilege, & Resistance'
eds. Heldke and O'Connor 2004.

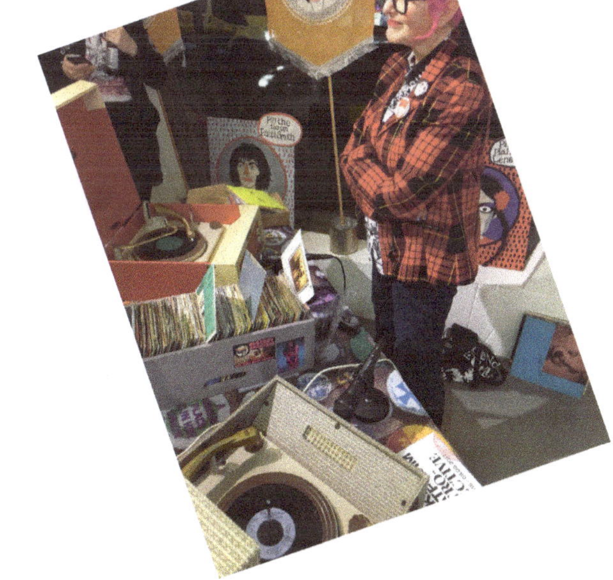

Rachael House with her **Feminist Disco** at Peckham Platform, London.

Why is this **so** important?

- Why *is* this important?

- I think that working-class people will never get beyond their bondage to capitalist relations unless they have their own cultures which are totally in their control and their artists are <u>completely free</u>.

- It's well-known that cultural repression was used as a basic weapon of imperialism, and to subdue slaves, but it's hard to see that it happened 'back at home' in a way that was so pervasive it became invisible.

- Why do we need culture? Isn't it just a luxury, an escape and so on? Well it can be that, but at its core, culture is the means by which we evaluate our totality, by playing using all our senses and coming to new concepts.

- Getting beyond capitalism is going to need new thinking, new social relations and and a new self-confidence. That level of innovation is only gonna be reached through freely improvised play. It's not gonna be achieved by screwing up our brow and thinking with brain alone.

- I think that the reason why working-class people can't reach out to each other for the solidarity that would allow them to think and take control of their own cultural spaces, as a prelude to taking control of everything, is because we have had generations of cultural repression, and also a dependence on other basic provisions through the municipalisation of town life. Culture that is part of social relations is a means to renegotiate the shared values that underpin solidarity.

- Contemporary cultural institutions and spaces have very little to do with us and are certainly not set up to help us liberate ourselves from oppression (quite the opposite). The ways in which we *have* taken initiatives have not been recognised and defended by unions or working-class organisations.

- I've been trying to look at how this happened; how people resisted and to suggest some limited (new) ideas of how we might strike back against the system (or perhaps ignore it?).

- Culture is integrated with language and with thinking. But cultural play can also communicate across language and other differences. Recent work with The Scratch Orchestra's Improvisation Rites, in the South of France, have shown this to me. A diverse group of students and local residents were able to improvise together beautifully, simply by agreeing on some simple verbal images as a starting place.

Amateur film, home movies and artists film

Another area of working-class culture I've looked into is amateur film and home movies. Something that has recently expanded exponentially with the smart phone and online platforms.

In the post-war period there was a dramatic rise in consumer wealth and a subsequent expansion of suburban living. In 1952 6% of US families had a movie camera but this was to rise rapidly throughout the fifties and sixties as cheaper 8mm foreign cameras flooded the market, even forcing the mighty Bell and Howell out of amateur camera production by 1962. Amateur film on 8mm was denigrated by film writers of the time as substandard, worthless and unwatchable. Amateur film-makers were constantly directed to imitate Hollywood's narrative conventions - advice that was consistently ignored. Amateur 8mm film technique seemed to be typified by some of the following methods:

1   Shooting whatever takes your fancy within the constraints of a limited footage. (A reel is just under four minutes). This tends to make the filmic relation to perception transparent.
2   Flash panning and fire hosing. This means the camera follows eye movements. The effect achieved is anti-illusory, fore-fronting the presence and spontaneous will of the camera operator.
3   Lack of planning. Having chronological rather scripted narrative intentions. Recording experience as an end in itself.
4   No editing. Giving a sense of an unmediated record or memory and making the production process evident.

One of the values of home movies is as an ethnographic record, with the crucial difference that they are unmediated self-representations, rather than those of a professional ethnographer. But home movies are also, to a greater or lesser extent, works of art in their own right. Unusually this was widely recognised by the experimental film artists in the US underground in the fifties and sixties. These artists used the techniques of working class film culture but it did not lead to a general liberation of film culture within the working-classes. There seem to have been no strong lines of communication between these bohemian artists and the wider working-class communities. In my experience in the UK with the open access film group Exploding Cinema, whom I made a study of from 1997 to 2002, the same thing is true to a greater or lesser degree. There is a lack of vibrant connection to working-class communities and a paucity of critical reflection on the films and videos that are shown.

Exploding Cinema offer *to show anything* that is sent to them and in many other ways have an inclusive and welcoming structure.

The lack of critical discourse on home movies means that they can easily be dismissed as having little value, once they have left the localised (often family) context in which they are made. The connections to their historical significance are difficult to draw spontaneously, even if you are knowledgeable about working-class history and culture. One of the things that needs to be done within working-class culture is that we need to find a way to talk about it - as audience and as artists. To become conscious of it as cultural work/play. Perhaps in a somewhat formal way that seems to make people feel a bit uncomfortable!

I have tried something like this with performing Agit Disco. People are invited to bring just one track each to a public meeting to share and to talk about why they chose it. This has worked remarkably well in a variety of settings, from an art gallery to a pub.

My doctoral thesis 'Exploding Cinema 1991 - 1997' (RCA 2002) is no longer online but will be made available as a book later in 2020.

"Calls for the best writers often accompanied demands for the uplift of the industry. The trade press urged the motion picture industry to legitimate itself by producing scenarios penned by well-known writers of fiction and drama. In 1908, for example, the New York Dramatic Mirror ran an article by a 'moving picture enthusiast' who strenuously advocated 'a higher class of authorship in the construction of plots or stories' as opposed to the 'crudest kind of drama' and 'the lowest kind of slapstick comedy', which had hitherto dominated. Stories produced by higher-class authors would appeal to the 'more intelligent class of spectators'. (Uricchio & Pearson 1993 p.46)

It was not until 1904 that the first purpose-built 'electric palaces' made their appearance. By 1925 the USA had nearly a thousand opulent 'picture palaces' - no longer simple halls but buildings of spectacular opulence which rivalled the best theatres. By this time the cinema audience in the USA alone had reached around 50 million a week, with the industry increasingly centred on Hollywood. As 'talking pictures' developed into the 1930s the cinema was now increasingly favoured by the middle classes.

The ever larger sums of money to be made also brought mass-market film firmly under the control of the capitalist class. They imported their own literary culture by way of the script and the aesthetics of good taste. The Charlie Chaplin films of the 1920's can be seen as a bridge to this period. His influences from working class culture and music hall met a Hollywood system which had an ethos of respectability and taste, and a literary heritage. As commercial cinema evolved through the 1930's and 1940s it increasingly relied on **the film-script**. The content was respectable and sentimental. The illusion of narrative continuity was smooth. There was a sheen of perfection which created an increasing gulf from the self-generated activity of amateur film-makers. This industrial dominance of good taste was maintained until there was a resurgence of the vulgar in the form of B-Movie horror, rock and sex genres in the consumer explosion of the 1950's.

For Everard M. Phillips recent Trinidadian political calypso is something as serious as your life. He ascribes to it a direct role in a 'non-formal' process of jurisprudence, or what he prefers to call 'conflict transformation'. His ideas on conflict transformation draw on studies of globally widespread practices of dispute resolution by informal mediation, challenging the literary approach to law that is built into the history of western states and their courts. Phillips defines conflict as 'an inevitable part of the triadic process of learning, growth and change' (p.17): he prefers the idea of a transformation of meanings to that of 'conflict resolution', which often ends up resolving a problem in a way that brings more advantages to one party – usually the state – than the subaltern other, thus reproducing the original inequalities. It is also clear from the beginning that Phillips includes class, gender, and race oppression in his idea of conflict. This theoretical knowledge is enriched by the author's own experience of working as a mediator.

In the original **Agit Disco** project I proposed people make playlists of music that had played a political part in their lives. I had taken the showing of music's role in political will formation as the goal. In reality, political will formation leads to taking power, legislation and the administration of social justice or law. Phillips made me realise that law can be re-conceptualised in ways that are very different from the legal system I took for granted. The process of conflict transformation, that he argues culture can contribute to, is something I recognise from the area known as therapeutic knowledge but had not before thought of in relation to a rethinking of legality.

Although this is arguably not the product of an urban working class, it _is_ the product of proletarians and is a great example of how music can participate directly in a democratic and quasi-legal discourse.

- This book has been mainly about music and song. But of course cultures exist in many art forms that roughly equate to the human senses. I have touched on movie making.

- I have taken a life-long interest into the repression of the working class ability to built itself sufficient and excellent housing. Before and outside of capitalism people just built houses from the locally available materials to meet housing needs. No problem! 10% of working class people currently work in the construction industry, but even more have building skills that are more than adequate to make housing for their community.

- In the UK we can see a currently surviving ability to build shelter in the making of sheds. Improvisation and recycling are a valued part of the shed aesthetic. Aye, there is working class culture there as well as an objective fulfilment of a need and an economic imperative.

- A similar improvised building process was used in a widespread plotland movement from the 1920s to the 1960s. I tell the story of how this was repressed from above in my previous book *The Conspiracy of Good Taste*.

- Recently I made a photographic study of two surviving plotlands on the Gower Peninsula in South Wales. I was trying to depict the way these evolved over time and in relation to planning authorities, and to give an honest representation of what they are like, rather than going for a 'cabin porn' approach by choosing only the prettiest and quirkiest examples. This study is published as: *Chalet Fields of the Gower* available as hardback or ebook.

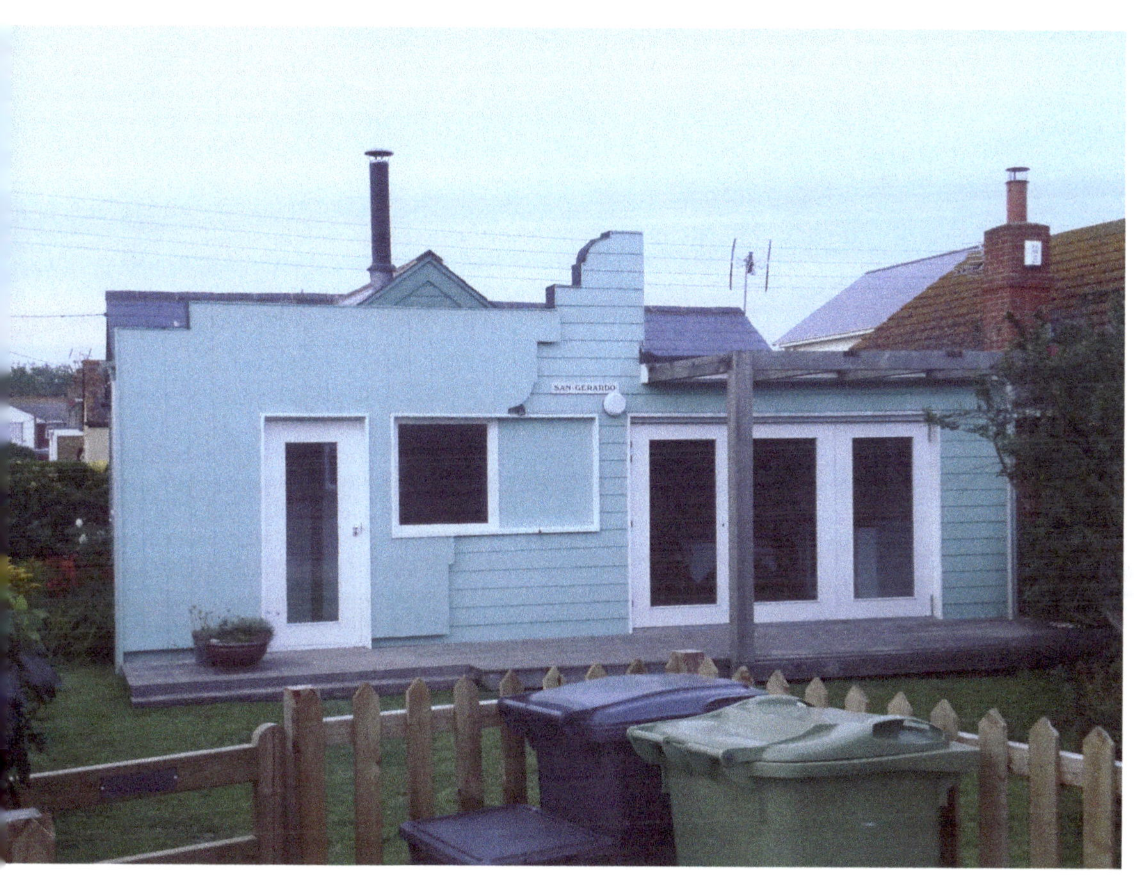

Plotland house, with a postmodern flourish, on the English south coast.

When I did my MA in 1996 the college library had a set of the *British Journal of Aesthetics*. I searched through these for any articles about 'popular culture' of any kind. I was shocked to find nothing until c1987. Further searches found that the first defence of popular culture, as having positive value was made by the sociologist Herbert J. Gans (b.1927) in his book, *Popular Culture and High Culture,* (1974).

Then from c1987 Richard Shusterman, a US philosopher (b.1949), wrote consistently about popular culture and aesthetics, some of which appeared in the British Journal of Aesthetics. Shusterman's first book on the subject was *Pragmatist Aesthetics: Living beauty, Rethinking Art,* (1992) and it has been translated into 14 languages.

It took me days of sitting in a library, looking through a great pile of dry journals, for it to sink in quite what I was up against as a working-class artist. The barrier that I couldn't see, but only feel, was not a phantom it had a basis in real exclusions and systematic absences in published discourses and the archive which had only begun to be challenged a very few years before. Perhaps this kind of insight can only be gained through struggle and I won't be able to persuade you of it here?

Emmanuelle Cooper (1938 - 2012) was the only person I knew at that time who was approaching this problem head on. He had an ambitious project called 'The People Art' (resulting in a book of the same name). He was hoping to establish a national museum of working class art. Much of what he found was already languishing unseen in museum basements. The only thing was, he defined a 'working-class artist' as someone who hadn't been to art college. I thought that this definition made his collection much less challenging. However, the establishment still completely ignored his proposal.

In spite of Shusterman's book being published globally there is still a class divide between popular and fine art.

According to Richard Shusterman, one of the most pressing sociocultural problems of today is the aesthetic legitimisation of popular art. He feels that though popular art may now *seem* to be socially justified, its artistic value is still questioned and demoted, which leads to the following problems:

- Popular art is "deprived of artistic care and control" which could protect it against the negative influence of the market, and, as a result, it often becomes "brutally crude in sensibility" From 'Pragmatist Aesthetics' p.168

- Satisfactions provided by this kind of art cannot be complete since they are diminished by a sense of humiliation which is induced in its audience by official art institutions' explicit disapproval of popular art forms.

- This situation in turn "intensifies painful divisions in society and even in ourselves". from 'Popular Art and Education', *Studies in Philosophy and Education*, 13, 1995, p. 203

In her book **Artful Science: enlightenment entertainment and the eclipse of visual education**, (1994) Barbara Stafford argues convincingly that there was a popular visual pedagogy in the early C17th. This often took the form of performance in which advances in science and technology were brought to public notice by, often spectacular, and nearly always entertaining demonstrations. The erstwhile performer might use their own body to dramatically demonstrate things such as the properties of electricity! These sorts of performances happened not only in institutes but in fairs, coffee houses and other places where people gathered to be entertained and informed. Going back much earlier the craftsmen, who drove the medieval industrial revolution that produced the technologies of windmills and sailing ships, would communicate their ideas with demonstration pieces that they would lug around the country.

Images like conversation, proved to be maddeningly elusive and difficult to control. Power was at issue, especially when the producers of graphic designs claimed displays could be as instructive as texts and as entertaining as carnival shows. Barbara Stafford (1994) p.281. *This 'primitive' or representational dimension of communication - composed of dramatically enunciated iconic, metaphoric and symbolic messages- became increasingly undermined through disembodied data caste in lead.* ibid p.196

Stafford shows how these ways of educating the public were undermined by the literary establishment. Pedagogical performances were made to seem like the illusions of cheap tricksters and magicians, and not worthy of the gravitas of serious learning. At the same time the literary culture of the middle class was continuing a long established process of separating itself from lower-class oral cultures.

The ability to find meaning in forms, colours, odours, and textures tended to disappear in the post-Lavoisier era of the 1780s, enamoured of quantifying set-ups. Stafford p.202

We see that working-class oral cultures tend towards an immersion in visual means of communication. At the same time the academic world of the universities saw visual communication as being below the remit of serious knowledge, which was a literary affair. The fewer pictures a book had the more serious it was etc. *The playful combinations of meaning invited by the cabinet of curios was replaced by systematically organised bits that required 'the interpretation of experts'.* Stafford p.255

A note on:

Barbara Ehrenreich, 'Dancing in the Streets: a history of collective joy', 2007

We are reminded that the first self-discipline required at school is the ability to inhibit bodily movement and to sit still for hours. Ehrenreich argues that moving together as a group is a profound motor of human connection/ communitas/ collectivity/ and commun-ity. First, she looks at how religious ritual functioned in this way. She describes early Christianity as being a danced religion which was repressed by the Romans. Later, as the Christian church develops its own hierarchy and power elite, dancing in churches is stopped by the church authorities themselves. This culminates in the edicts of Calvin, the suspicion of the sensual and the 'Protestant work ethic' that was so useful to capitalism.

She suggests that social separation and physical pacification may lead to all kinds of ills. She describes the limitations of Freud who could only imagine a sexually charged love between two persons and had not experienced or conceived of group bonding by moving together, much less anything approaching collective ecstasy.

She observes a basic pattern by which repression occurs. Firstly the elite themselves withdraw from the festivities. The festivities continue for a while without them, but then they present a challenge to power and are repressed. Is it possible that positive somatic effects of the Rave dance scene of the late Eighties will be evident, as those who took part in it come into positions of greater social influence? This should be happening around about now! Have the progressive leaders of the future been formed in the anti-globalisation carnivals of the recent past?

We all know how schools and armies hate 'fidgeting' bodies... but Barbara Ehrenreich suggests **the repression of movement** has been tied up with the subjugation of the crowd long before modern urbanisation and mass education.

Bibliography

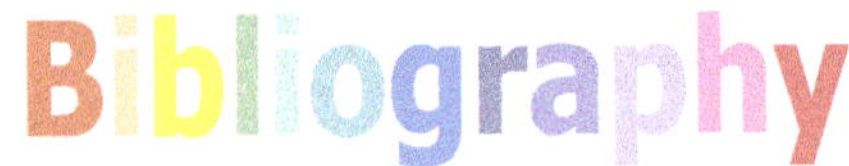

Cooper, Emmanuel. *People's Art: working class art from 1750 to the present day*, Mainstream 1994

Della Fave, L. Richard. 'The Psychology of Culture: making oppression appear normal',
A review of Carl Ratner's book, *Macro Cultural Psychology: A Political Philosophy of Mind*
(Oxford UP, 2011) in Monthly Review, January 2013

Ehrenreich, Barbara. *Dancing in the Streets: a history of collective joy*, Granta 2007

Gans, Herbert J. *Popular Culture and High Culture*, Basic Books 1974

George, Michele. quoted in Victoria Moon Joyce, *Bodies that sing: The formation

of singing subjects*, PhD. Thesis, University of Toronto 2003

Hale, Susan. *Song and Silence: voicing the soul*, La Alameda Press 1995

Kidson, Frank. *A Garland of English Folk-songs*. Collected and edited by Frank Kidson
with pianoforte accompaniments by Alfred Moffat, Ascherberg Hopwood & Crew Ltd 1926

Moon Joyce, Victoria. 'Turn Off the Radio and Sing for Your Lives',

from Karen Warren's *Women's Voices in Experiential Education*, Kendall Hunt 1996

Phillips, Everard M. *The Political Calypso: a sociolinguistic process of conflict transformation*, Port of Spain 2009

Rancière, Jacques, *Aesthesis: scenes from the aesthetic regime of art*, Verso 2013

Sharp, Cecil J. and S. Baring Gould. *English Folk Songs for Schools*, Curwen edition, 1908

Sharp, Cecil J. *English Folk Song: some conclusions*, (Orig. 1907) Mercury Books (4th Edition) 1965

Shusterman, Richard. *Pragmatist Aesthetics: living beauty, rethinking art*, Blackwell, 1992

Small, Christopher. *Musicking: the meanings of performing and listening*, Wesleyan U.P. 1998

Solnit, Rebecca. 'The Mother of All Questions', Harpers Magazine, October 2015

Standford, Charles Villiers. Ed. *The National Song Book*, Boosey & Co 1906

Szczelkun, Stefan. *The Conspiracy of Good Taste*, (2nd edition) Routine Art Co 2017

Uricchio, William. and Roberta E. Pearson. *Reframing Culture: The Case of the Vitagraph
Quality Films*, Princeton U.P. 1993

Williams, Raymond. *Culture and Society: 1780 - 1950*, Chatto and Windus 1958

Young, Iris. 'Five Faces of Oppression', in *Oppression, Privilege, & Resistance*,
eds. Lisa Heldke & Peg O'Connor; Mcgraw Hill 2004

I realise this booklet is full of half-explored ideas but I think it is only by working class people talking together in person, and listening carefully to each others thinking, (and rage?), that we will come to a better understanding of how class oppression has been channeled through culture and how we can reverse this situation.

If you would like to have a constructive discussion about the materials assembled in this booklet please *contact me* by email: stefan@ukart.com or via social media.

I would like to meet up with people who have been thinking about working class culture.

Longer reviews of books in the latter part of this publication can be found on my blog: http://stefan-szczelkun.blogspot.com

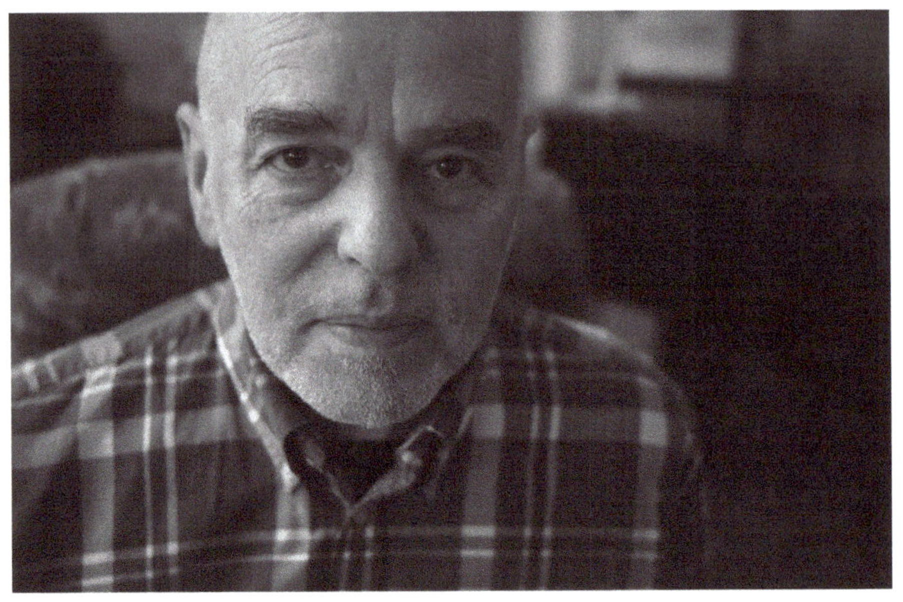

Photo of the author by Maya Szczelkun   January 2020

The author would like to thank the following people who wrote such thoughtful endorsements after reading a PDF of the draft: Jennet Thomas, Karen Strang, Valerie Walkerdine, Rachael House, Jacky Lansley, Lorraine Leeson, Diane Reay, Paul Jamrozy, Jordan McKenzie... Thanks to Tim Kahn for proof reading.